YOUTH IN TROUBLE

A SYMPOSIUM: May 2 and 3, 1974
Airport Marina Hotel
Dallas-Fort Worth Regional Airport

Edited By Betty Lou Kratoville

Academic Therapy Publications
1539 Fourth Street
San Rafael, California 94901

International Standard
Book Number: 0-87879-096-9

Library of Congress
Catalog Card Number: 74-29559

Cover Design: James H. Wallace

This book was set in IBM
Press Roman 11 point medium
and medium italic type.
Chapter titles were set in
Varityper 24 point Garamond bold.
Other titles were set in 16 point
Garamond bold. The paper used
was 50 pound Bookwhite for the
text; 10 point CIS for the cover.

Printed in the
United States of America

Table of Contents

This book is dedicated to the "planners."
They recognized the need,
and they will not rest
until the world recognizes it, too.

Chester Poremba
John and Lee Ida Wacker
Pat Schwartz
John R. Moss
Eleanor Martin
Graham Clark
Leora Harrison

. . . and a special thanks to Marge Elste who
transcribed all the tapes.

Co-Hosting Organizations

Area Councils, Texas Association for Children with Learning Disabilities
Child Study Center of Fort Worth
Classroom Teachers of Dallas
League of Women Voters of Tarrant County
Mental Health Association of Dallas County
Mental Health Association of Tarrant County
National Council of Jewish Women (Greater Dallas Section)
Northwood Woman's Club of Dallas
Tarrant County Medical Education and Research Foundation
Texas Association for Services to Children
Texas Easter Seal Society
Women's Council of Dallas County
YMCA (Metropolitan Dallas)

Introduction

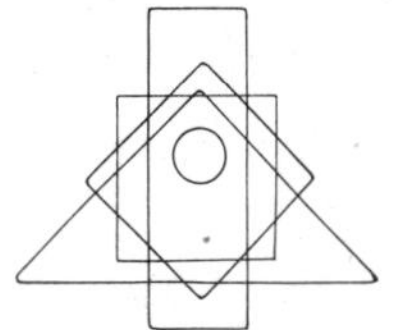

A current popular pastime, both in the parlor and at the podium, is amazement (raised eyebrows) and disapproval (small clucking sounds) over the staggering rise in crimes committed by juveniles. Like inclement weather, everyone has talked about juvenile delinquency, but no one has done anything about it with the exception of a few, small, isolated endeavors which shine like tiny beacons in their own areas but which have done little to illuminate the national darkness.

Where does action in any great movement begin? Surely in the minds and hearts of men and women of vast commitment, huge concern, and giant intellect. It moves forward from recapitulation and review—"Where have we been and where are we now?"—to a sharing of ideas—"Where do we go from here?"

And so it was in Dallas in the spring of 1974 when men of ideas and action, representing education, medicine, psychology, and juvenile justice, gathered to discuss "Youth in Trouble."

Because this was a meeting of original minds, both on the platform and in the audience, healthy and altogether cordial disagreement was an integral part of the forum. Yet a concensus of opinion quickly emerged—i.e., adolescents are not properly nor humanely served in our educational and judicial systems. Education seems determined to push problem youngsters out rather than to keep them in as potentially productive citizens. Justice seems determined to keep them in rather than to push them out as potentially productive citizens. The net result, in terms of recidivism, is that more problem youngsters return to correctional institutions each year than return to school!

One could sense an urgency and an impatience and an indignation as the symposium speakers described and identified the problem and the youngsters, and grappled with solutions and alternatives.

It was a beginning and a good one! Representatives from the U.S. Department of Justice, who had come to listen and to learn, reeled under the impact of the message and urged that proceedings of the symposium be edited, published, and distributed throughout the land to juvenile judges, probation officers, educators, social workers, parents, and other concerned citizens.

An idea is reaching its moment in history. Hopefully, awareness of its importance, impact, and priority will be accelerated by the contents of this collection.

Betty Lou Kratoville,
Editor

What Are We About?
Come, Let's Counsel Together.

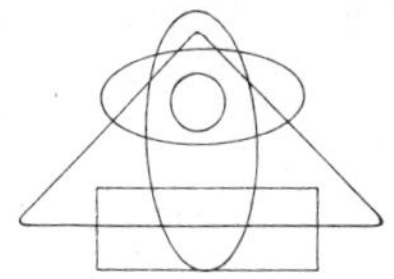

This is a signal honor for me. I don't know how many people in their professions reach this kind of experience, a fruition of a life's dream. One other miracle that I witnessed in my practice came during the course of treatment of a blind man, forty eight years old, who had been blind for forty of those years. I watched him restored to full sight by the modern miracle of surgery, and it blew my mind for the next year! This symposium is probably going to blow my mind for the rest of my life!

Video tapes of this meeting will be distributed to two hundred and twenty cities in the United States. I have an idea they will ultimately be distributed to many countries across both oceans. In addition to audio and visual tapes, we hope to have a number of publications—a book, proceedings, manuals—for people in the various professions, particularly juvenile court judges.

Our distinguished group of speakers, all professionals, come from many walks of life. We have representatives from psychology, medicine, probation, education. Many of the speakers you will hear today and tomorrow have written books, have been in the field for a long time, each in his own interest, but all talking about "Youth in Trouble." Those of us in learning disabilities have heretofore been focusing our attention on the pre-school child, the elementary school child, and early identification. Today we are going to change our emphasis. We are going to talk about the kids who grow up. Ogden Nash once said,

> "The trouble with a kitten is that
> It eventually grows up to be a cat!"

Our kids do grow up, and what happens to them is very serious business because they are human, even as you and I. In terms of an operational model, we will be discussing a group of troubled youth, but as we talk about them, we will be talking about the needs of all mankind and certainly about the needs of the adolescents in this country who comprise approximately 60 percent of the total census.

The message today, ladies and gentlemen, is that we are taking a big step into a new era. We are going to start taking a look at what happens to kids at the secondary level or, more truthfully, what doesn't happen to them. I want to tell you a story which has a moral. A warden of a state penitentiary was booked a year in advance to speak at the next state convention of judges. In the intervening year between booking and actuality, "Statesville" had a number of riots and upheavals. Pretty soon the judges in the state were taking potshots at the warden in the newspapers. On the day the warden was to speak at the banquet, a nervous hush fell over the crowd because everyone knew that he would now be speaking to the very people who had been so critical. When he stood up, the hush got even hushier, and he said, "My dear judges and ladies and gentlemen, as you know, we have been having some trouble at Statesville. Some of you have taken some pretty good licks at me in the newspapers, some even suggesting I should be fired. What you don't understand is that we are very interested in what is happening in Statesville, too, because we live there and have a vested interest in what is going on. My staff and I have just spent three months studying the problems of Statesville. We have put in many hours and lots of overtime and just this morning we had our final meeting at which conclusions of our study were drawn. That's the meeting I left to come here to speak to you, so you will be the first public audience to hear the results of our study." And the hush got even hushier. He continued, "We have found out what is causing all those riots at Statesville. The reason we are having so many problems, so much trouble, so many riots, is that you guys ain't too fussy about whom you send there!" The moral of my story is that heretofore we really ain't been too fussy about whom we send into secondary schools or out into the world. We hope to bridge that gap today.

by
Chester Poremba

"Who Are These Children? Learning Disabilities Defined."

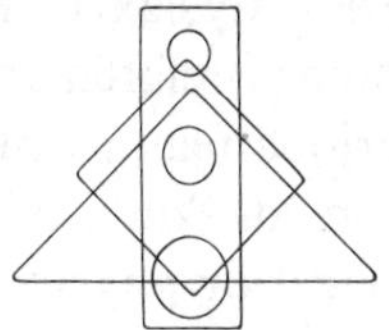

The child with specific learning disability fails to perform up to expectation in the regular classroom in spite of average or even superior intelligence, normal vision and hearing, and a home environment conducive to stable emotional adjustment and affording stimulating incentive to learning. Once considered a relatively uncommon finding, learning disability is now recognized to involve as many as twenty percent of the entire school population. Increased understanding of the involved child has shown that in addition to his classroom difficulties, he has disorders of activity and attention control as well as behavior and thought. This constellation is now referred to as minimal brain dysfunction, a syndrome which reflects developmental immaturity of the central nervous system related to a biochemical insufficiency affecting the integrity of function of the reticular matter in the brain stem and its connections to the limbic brain and other basal structures.

The activity disorders include hyperactivity or hypoactivity, gross and fine motor incoordination with clumsiness and apraxia, and sleep problems. In the area of behavior and thought the child with minimal brain dysfunction shows a short attention span and distractibility, perseveration, memory difficulties, especially for material presented sequentially, perceptual-concept disorders, poor abstract reasoning, and disorganization, and is emotionally unstable. In the classroom he has particular difficulty with the communicating skills: reading (dyslexia), writing (dysgraphia) and math (dyscalculia), and often shows inordinate problems in transferring his knowledge to the written page.

Because of prejudice and misunderstanding the learning disabled child has been the victim of mismanagement of many of those who deal with him. The hyperactive child who does not sit still in the classroom may be considered spoiled or acting out his hostility to parental mismanagement, while the withdrawn hypoactive child is often called lazy or underachieving. His awkwardness and clumsiness are likely to make him an object of scorn and derision by his classmates so that he becomes a loner on the playground. The short attention span and distractibility are often misinterpreted as indicating the child is nervous, probably due to discord at home, while the memory difficulties are considered to indicate willful disobedience or poor study habits which require punishment or more pressure. The concept disorders and poor abstraction are often felt to indicate that the child has deep-seated emotional problems rooted in early childhood trauma, again blamed on the parents.

Understanding of the actual learning disorders have also been fraught with misconceptions by those who have failed to look at the whole child. The very term "dyslexia" has been misinterpreted to indicate some form of esoteric brain damage related to mixed or incomplete hemispheric dominance or pathology in various regions of the brain similar to that seen in adults who have lost the ability to read. When conventional examination failed to disclose evidence of true neurological or physical involvement, it was naturally assumed that the disorder had to be functional or psychosomatic in nature. Others would blame the entire problem on the newer methods of teaching reading, or on crowded classrooms, or on poorly trained teachers, or on the inconsistencies of the English language itself. Costly programs for the elimination of learning disability have been proposed based on the assumption that socio-cultural deprivation is the only factor involved, and that elimination of poverty will automatically insure the disappearance of learning disability.

Meanwhile, investigators seem to be unaware of the seriousness of the problems of learning disability as they involve a wide spectrum of school population in all classes, in numbers so large as to constitute the most prevalent of all chronic disorders of childhood, nor do they seem to be willing to accept the fact that failure in school may well have the most devastating effect of all experiences on the developing child's personality.

Once the vicious circle becomes established, the learning disabled child is pressured and humiliated by his teachers, punished and often rejected by his parents, and taunted and ridiculed by his classmates. He becomes desperate for acceptance by his peers and in his search for approval he may become the classroom clown, or a grandiose and boastful liar, or he may resort to stealing in his efforts to buy recognition. His immaturity soon allows him to become the scapegoat who is blamed for nearly every misdeed that occurs, so that his reputation is now firmly established. He comes to realize that he is trapped in an unyielding educational system in which he must compete with his peers who possess skills and talents which are denied to him. His years of failure and nonacceptance crush his self-esteem and his school experiences leave him bitter and defiant, or withdrawn and defeated.

Fortunately, knowledge is now at hand to reverse this trend and bring help to the learning disabled child that is long overdue. Recognition that the greater majority of affected children are boys and that there is a high incidence of involvement in other members of the family points to a sex-linked familial disorder. The remarkable response to stimulant medication which often produces an almost unbelievable improvement in classroom performance, in behavior, and in self-esteem points to a biochemical basis.

Increased understanding of the chemical relationship to attention, behavior, memory and actual learning assure further research to bring added equipment to the medical therapeutic armamentarium in the future. This, together with early recognition, increased flexibility of educational curricula, and proper remedial tutorial efforts when indicated hold promise for a much brighter future for the learning disabled child. When every kindergarten and elementary school teacher understands learning disability and recognizes her role in the early recognition and management of these children, the greater majority of the learning disabled will be salvaged during their early years of school and will be retained in the mainstream of regular educational channels where they belong.

by
Harold Levy

Characteristic Symptom Patterns of Learning Disabled Adolescents

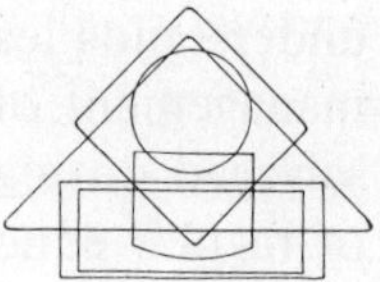

I have been directly involved in evaluating, setting up programs, and following the progress of young people with learning disabilities for a long time. Until a few years ago, a meeting of this sort would have been inconceivable, even gauche, because the early work of the great pioneers in learning disabilities was focused upon early identification and early adequate provision of services. Invariably, this effort, whenever it seemed successful, was accompanied by the unspoken aspiration or hope that such early intervention would give rise to correction which would eventuate in fully normal development and adequate adaptiveness to social circumstances.

Today and tomorrow we are talking about the adolescent with learning disabilities because we have found that the hopes of the early great figures in this field, with many of whom I had the pleasure of being associated, have not been fully borne out in experience. We continue to see that learning disabled individuals who have displayed all of the characteristics described by Dr. Levy continue to have some form of difficulty into adolescence and young adulthood. Even where we have had the good fortune of providing every available facility to these youngsters by way of identification and treatment and programming, there are still problems which crop up. There are subtle vestiges of earlier difficulties which have not been fully assuaged nor fully remediated.

We know that there is no single pattern of behavior, no single identifiable, clear-cut, narrow gauge symptom pattern that is attributable to every learning disabled young person. There are deficits and shortcomings which have continued with the child all through his life in perception, in motor development, in attention, in memory, in language. However, these often take a different form, a more subtle and sometimes more insidious form, as the child grows older. One of the major difficulties which the learning disabled adolescent and young adult face is the very fact that he does not have a clearly discernible handicap, one that is readily visable to everyone—parents, friends, relatives, people in the greater community. These children are not like deaf or retarded or cerebral palsied youngsters. For the most part they look and act normal or average enough so it is easy to overlook or discount their difficulties. Therefore, because of their lack of an easily identifiable problem, a symptom pattern, they do not evoke the understanding and the sympathy and the tolerance that other young people with difficulties experience, and people are not very nice to them as they grow into adolescence. Sometimes people have been fairly nice to them when they were young kids because they were attractive, they were cute, and they were still full of promise. In some ways, we saw evidence of abilities and aptitudes which we wanted to bring to fruition, and we tried to set them up in helpful programs. But, invariably, they grow older.

I have had the good fortune, sometimes highly rewarding and on other occasions painful, to follow almost two thousand young people with learning disabilities into adolescence and young adulthood. I can't keep in touch with every one of them, but I try to, and there are many, many young people whom I have continued to see over a ten year period. Some are in their mid twenties now, and I am still seeing them, working with them, talking with them, and following their progress with a great, great deal of interest. My friends on the panel know I like to tell stories, and this lack of a readily identifiable clear-cut pattern of which we have been speaking reminds me of several old, retired Jewish gentleman sitting at Miami Beach together. They are sitting around, thinking about their past lives and what they have experienced. Some feel they have accomplished a great deal, and others feel that they have done very little. One old gentleman, who is very depressed, very apathetic, very lethargic, says, "In my life I have accomplished so little as I look back. Nothing that I can really see. I'm nothing. I'm *nothing!*" One of his friends turns to the others and says, "Look at Sam. Look who thinks he's nothing!" In other words, even the concept that he hadn't accomplished anything, his dependence on others for sympathy and awareness and support, was denied this man. So many of our young people seem to feel this way. I talked to a thirteen year old recently who has been through the kinds of experiences and frustration and defeat which we have heard described and who epitomized his reaction to all of this by saying, "Boy! God sure goofed when he put me together!"

These young people continue to present some kind of uneven profile of development, a pattern of irregular and erratic and inconsistent maturation which makes them highly puzzling to others because of the continuing gaps in some of their skills, because of their difficulties in associating with others, because of their inability to set forth plans and programs for themselves and follow these with consistency. One mother of a teen-aged boy told me recently, "You know, my boy has a lot going for him. There is so much he has. He's got everything that everybody else has but somehow it's not wrapped tight." She had the feeling that he was loose and diffuse and all over the lot.

However, as I shall stress today and tomorrow, along with this inconsistency, this scattered profile, this unevenness of maturation, comes miraculously, in almost every case, a sudden outcropping of something which wasn't anticipated when the child was young–some flare, some talent, some skill, which could not be forecast from early work with these youngsters. As I say repeatedly, I have very rarely seen a learning disabled youngster who does not somehow, if given the advantages of early appropriate education and family understanding and community support, come through with a sudden, almost startingly unexpected flare which we must, as I will say again and again, identify, encourage, and nurture in every way we possibly can. One youngster I heard about last night suddenly out of the blue has developed an enormous interest in the lives of American presidents dating back to the beginning of our history. His mother told the delightful anecdote of his coming home from school with a library book held behind his back. "This week I'm going to do a book report on sports," he announced, grinning. "What?" she responded. "You mean you aren't going to report on one of the presidents?" He held up the book–*Sports of Our Presidents!*

Other kids love to make models, other kids love to whittle, other kids like to fool around with machinery, other kids develop a sudden literary talent. It is true that many of the youngsters with whom we are concerned are limited in regard to the efficiency skill of verbal expression, both in speaking and in writing, but, curiously, I have encountered quite a few who have suddenly come through, despite evidence of early learning difficulty, in the language area. Come through with startling creativity in the area of writing poetry, in setting forth short stories, in giving vent to their fantasies through artistic endeavor. Many, many of our youngsters with learning disability come through as having abilities in the arts and crafts, areas that were not anticipated early in their life and seemed, in fact, to be counterindicated. The same child who could not write his name very well or could not line up numbers in an even column suddenly is immensely gifted in terms of sculpture, modeling, and artistic endeavors of various kinds.

It is terribly important to identify those areas in which the child is unimpeded, unobstructed, because the feeling exists that as our kids get older, there is some mysterious obstruction, some barrier, to their full achievement and that, all of a sudden, they stumble and fall in unaccountable ways. This is often true because the continuing difficulty in many of the learning disabled children is processing and reacting to information from the environment. I would like to broaden the idea of communication handicap beyond the narrow confines of that which I am concerned with as a speech therapist, an audiologist, a remedial reading specialist, into difficulty in picking up, assessing, and giving proper weight to all kinds of social cues. One of the major barriers to the full social realization of the learning disabled child as he grows to be a teen-ager is that he doesn't pick up and interpret cues which we all take as implicit and which are given in every social situation–clues like when you meet someone, how you look at them, how you shake hands, how close you stand to them, how loud your voice should be. In many cases, the voice of a learning disabled adolescent is too loud for a particular situation or not loud enough. They shout or they mumble–one or the other. You know, you go for an interview, and you sit, and you talk, questions are asked, and all of a sudden you see from a subtle shift of body, that the interview is terminated. The person doesn't say, "Well, we've done enough of this, we've had enough talk, goodbye now." But he moves forward in his chair and indicates he is about to get up and say, "Well, thank you for the opportunity of talking with you, it's been very nice meeting you, etc." It's this kind of subtle, little cueing that everyone of us gets from everybody else in every single social situation that these children fail to process and act upon.

In a way, this could be considered as a difficulty in integrating in three levels. First, a difficulty in integrating information to which you have been previously exposed to the present situation, how you weigh and put together, how you integrate all of the information from all of your social contacts and all of your activities throughout your life and bring all of that to bear upon the immediate situation. That's something these youngsters have difficulty with—pulling in from the past and acting upon previous information. Secondly, there's also the immediate situation, how you identify those subtle cues, facial expressions, bodily attitudes, voice cues, which, in fact, occupy about 40 percent of all our time when we're talking to each other because only 60 percent of any message in any communicative situation is borne by the actual content of the words. A great deal of information is borne by subtleties of vocal inflections, bodily postures, facial expressions, a lift of the eyebrow, a turn of the body, and this is what the kids don't get. Then, a different kind of integration takes place over time, an ability to judge what is needed to take from the present situation that can be transposed into the future for appropriate decisions and proper action. One of the difficulties of these adolescents is their kind of innocence, naivete, guilelessness, heedlessness, because they are not sure what they can pick up from the present situation which can be carried over into the future.

All of this, then, gives rise to the following kinds of difficulties—a relative lack of ability to adapt to situations in even the very bright adolescent and young adult, a lack of resourcefulness, a lack of ability to count upon one's own qualities and attributes to adapt flexibly to new situations. These youngsters, on their very narrow gauge track, find it difficult to consider alternatives—"What else might I do to tackle this problem?" "How else can I handle the situation or deal with these people, deal with these requirements or stresses and difficulties in which I find myself?" Such communication difficulties can be epitomized as poor ability to integrate and to adapt to situations so that the individual very frequently continues to find himself in embarrassing and humiliating circumstances where people are annoyed and irritated by him and find him upsetting. And the young people find themselves in this kind of situation to their own bewilderment because they know that their intentions are usually the best, they want to get along with people, they want to meet challenges, they want to adapt to circumstances, and they put forth their best efforts only to find that people turn from them, find them irritating, reject them, and do not concede their worth as human beings. This, then, of course feeds back constantly to reduce the individual's ability to form a sound stable identity and construct an image of himself as somebody who can be a worthy, acceptable, achieving individual. These young people almost invariably want to go out into the world, to get along with peers and authority figures, to make their way, to win acceptance, to make money, to marry, and to do everything everybody else does. Yet they find themselves repeatedly blocked by the kinds of deficits and ineptitudes and problems in interpreting, getting feedback from others and acting on this feedback, to the point that they are not constantly blamed.

In the past, there has been a kind of artificial separation, yielding only gradually and slowly, between the so-called emotional problems on the one hand and learning disabilities on the other, and this artificial kind of delineation is not borne out in experience in very many child guidance clinics and elsewhere. It is very rarely that a specific learning disability or perceptual handicap or language problem is not accompanied by difficulties in establishing a sense of identity and a feeling of worth and confidence. It is rarely a problem which comes to the attention of professionals of identity development, anxiety or regression, all supposed to be strictly emotional, where there is not a learning component. I believe there is a learning problem in most children who come to professional attention because in every case the child has not learned to get along with others, has not learned how to use his energies productively, has not been able to develop a sense of worth, and finds it very difficult to figure out how in the world he is going to carry responsibility, exercise good judgment, and achieve stature for himself in later life.

I am going to conclude with an optomistic note. In most instances, we can benefit these young people through identification and training. Some of these young people with learning disabilities are not the typical kids who come up through the ranks, so to speak, who were identified early. There are some learning disabled adolescents who don't appear until they reach the teen years and are suddenly identified because they haven't been able to make it in junior and senior high schools in the face of mounting pressures. But if we can identify these learning disabled adolescents, they will not retreat because of their sense of worthlessness to apathy, lethargy, passivity, or will not, on the other hand, vent their fury at the humiliations they have experienced all through their lives in anti-social behavior. They can be trained. Our attitude needs to be one of distinct hopefulness, that if we can provide them with gratifications, a sense of success, a feeling of worth, they will go forward and become productive citizens and happy individuals.

I'll conclude with a quotation I found just recently from Plato. Plato knew a lot about learning disabled persons and how to give them their due. He said, "Do not train boys to learning by force and harshness but direct them to it by what amuses and captures their minds so that you may be better able to discover, with accuracy, the peculiar bent of the genius of each child."

by
Milton Brutten

The Current State of the Art

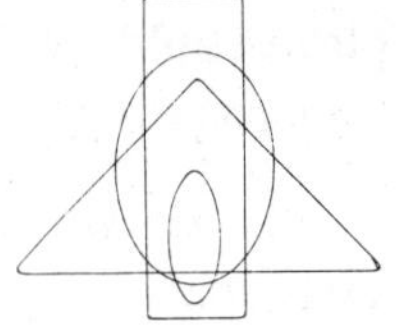

I have come to learning disabilities, to *general* problems of children, through research into the fraud we call our juvenile justice system in this country.

I met Tim about nine o'clock on a Saturday night. He was in the maximum security prison his state had for juveniles. It was a penitentiary—double set of walls, guard towers, high barbed wire. Tim was in the wing for the most troublesome boys in the place. He was in solitary confinement and had been for 71 of the 90 days immediately prior to my coming. He was also 12 years old. His major crime: an inability to control himself.

He had been a problem since he was nine months old, his mother told me later, a terror at home and school. He was totally unable to keep his temper. A boy called him "retard" in school one day. Tim, age twelve, stabbed him with a little penknife. That was the only thing he had ever done which could be construed as a criminal act. The court ordered him to a minimum security training school. He was so incorrigible that he was transferred to the maximum security jail.

In virtually every state in the country, you can move your way up in the juvenile prison system by simply being hard to handle. Unable to stop lashing out at virtually everyone around him, Tim spent most of his time in solitary confinement, a five by ten foot cell. When he was particularly troublesome, the cagemen injected him forcibly with Thorazine. Thorazine is a powerful tranquilizer. No physician ever prescribed Thorazine for treatment of Tim. The cagemen used the drug to keep him groggy. "One injection," they told me, "often keeps him out for six hours."

Tim was examined by a psychiatrist who reported, "This is a helpless little boy, confused and overwhelmed by his impulses. The next few years could be crucial as to whether he goes into irreversible personal disorder." The psychiatrist asked that Tim be given a medical evaluation and then treatment based on those findings. Four months later, the examination had not been scheduled. The same psychiatrist saw Tim again and again recommended the examination. When I last checked, Tim still had not received the evaluation and remained in jail, the victim of impulses he neither understood nor could control. He can remain in jail until he is eighteen when he may be released to carry his ungovernable impulses into society with him. And all the psychiatrist's requests lay neatly recorded in a file several inches thick.

I found Bernie in the detention home in an eastern state. The purpose of detention centers is to hold children temporarily until the court can make a judgment and a placement. Bernie was put there *at age six* for running away. But no place could be found for him. So he spent most of his next four years there, sitting in the day room watching television. A runaway among delinquents for four years.

He was frequently tested. At age six his IQ was well within the normal range. Two years later, the examining psychologist would report, "His contact with his environment has decreased." By nine, "Bernie is getting depressed. (He is) beginning to withdraw severely." At ten again the inevitable test. Bernie's IQ by now had plummeted 30 points. In four years! He was now retarded, the psychologist said. The juvenile court immediately and formally labeled him that and ordered him to a state institution for the retarded. Bernie had finally found a home. Six different sets of professionals had had a shot at Bernie during those four years. His probation department social worker (he was not a delinquent but he had a probation officer) and his school social worker had never even contacted each other to discuss his problems. I asked his probation department social worker what she did for him. "I visited him, and I brought him apples," she said. "He loved apples."

In another city, a seventeen year old girl, abandoned since she was ten and said to be emotionally disturbed, was taken *in handcuffs* to a barred cell in the maximum security ward for the criminally insane in a state hospital. She had no criminal charges pending against her and never did have. She had never seen a psychologist or a psychiatrist except for testing. Why is she *to this moment* in that hospital? I asked the judge who committed her, and he said, "What can be done? We have to accept the circumstances as they are."

In another state, a *five year old* boy who had set several fires was put into a jail for delinquents ages ten through eighteen. On no one's judgment other than that of a local magistrate! That state has a treatment center designed for children believed to be emotionally disturbed, but the psychiatrist in charge said it would take four to six weeks for the center staff to decide if it would accept him. At that point, the five year old had already been in the jail for four weeks. A newspaper reporter heard about the boy. He was moved two hours after the story appeared.

In still another city and state, a mother asked the court to help her with her fourteen year old son. She couldn't control him. To her amazement, the judge sentenced her son to a juvenile prison for three years "for rehabilitative treatment." The mother went to Legal Aid. A lawyer visited the boy and found he was spending all his time cutting the grass and watching television. He sued for release of the boy on the grounds that he was not getting the treatment that was the sole purpose for his being in jail. The state attorney general's office asked for and received a six month postponement of the hearing because of their backlog of work.

Three key facts tell much of our national juvenile delinquency story: (1) About six of every ten juvenile in jail—and I mean jail with locks and bars and guards—have committed *no* criminal acts. They are in trouble with their schools or victims of bad homes or no homes or runaways or mentally retarded or emotionally or physically handicapped or victims of health problems no one has bothered to hunt for. (2) Eight out of these same ten *do* commit crimes after they leave jail. (3) Some three out of four juveniles who are put in jail as juveniles are convicted of crime as adults.

We have no sure understanding of juvenile delinquency, yet we ignore most of what we do know. We are slowly beginning to realize that a great variety of children's problems have a physiological cause. Others today will speak directly to this point. But a small and growing group of physicians, researchers and others concerned with children who are delinquent suggest that organic reasons cause the behavior of some of them. Frequently, this behavior pattern often surfaces first as school problems, later, ignored, as problems outside of school.

"Our juvenile institutions today hold many youngsters who should not be detained," says a criminologist, "but who have been processed through the assembly line of juvenile jurisprudence without ever being seen by the competent person who could diagnose or even suggest evidence of a health impairment."

More than one million boys and girls are caught up in America's juvenile justice system each year. It is a ponderous machine that operates in secret and quickly and quietly disposes of a crushing burden of cases. The juvenile court is the *only* civilian court in this country which operates behind closed doors. The public is not admitted. In most cities, the press is excluded. The average hearing, according to the President's Crime Commission, takes five minutes. And as a result of such hearings, several hundred thousand children are jailed each year. On any day, *today,* more than one hundred thousand juveniles are behind bars.

Regardless of a child's problems, the juvenile court typically has two basic options available to it in disposition of a case: (1) Commitment to an institution; (2) Probation or discharge back to the family. Neither alone contributes to the *solution* of problems.

We need more options. Options in the form of the variety of responses necessary to juveniles who have a variety of problems. And, surely, one option must be the means to attempt to determine why that young person is before the judge.

"Whether a judge gives a kid a slap on the wrist or a harsh penalty, he'll be back," says psychologist Benedict Meyers, who specializes in juvenile crime problems, "unless someone explores *why* he's in trouble in the first place."

The President's Crime Commission said in 1967: "If pre-court services are given at all, they are generally inconsistent, haphazard, scattered among different agencies and fail to reach all children who need them. Records of serious, repeating offenders show that if badly needed services had been given when the youngster was *first* brought to public attention, *subsequent* delinquencies would have been reduced, if not eliminated."

Much more recently, the federal government's juvenile delinquency office said: "There is little coherent national planning or established priority structure among the programs dealing with delinquency prevention. There is a lack of effective national leadership. No model systems for the prevention of delinquency or the rehabilitation of delinquent youth have been developed or implemented.

There has been (no) feedback of knowledge, gained from research, for use in the development of such systems.

Tim, Bernie, and the several other children I spoke of a few moments ago are not isolated examples. They represent dozens of boys and girls I met across the country, *non*-delinquent children who are committed to institutions for indeterminate stays under the guise of treatment. But, according to the National Council on Crime and Delinquency, only five out of one hundred get it.

No one, anywhere, demands an accounting of what happens to these children. Nobody touches their lives. Except on a hit or miss basis, no hand exists to support a stumbling child, no hand exists to help good families who find survival impossible without assistance. I interviewed parents of troubled children who committed their children to juvenile courts, in desperation because they could find no other promise of treatment. Each child went to jail as an alleged incorrigible. None got the promised treatment.

Logic plays little part in our treatment of children in trouble. We imprison a child of seven and tell ourselves he is the failure. We maintain we will treat him, but only one of twenty institution employees is assigned to rehabilitation. We worry about the rising rate of crime and acknowledge that serious juvenile crime is up sharply (half of all major crimes are committed by juveniles), yet our federal government spent $14 million for delinquency prevention the last year I looked—versus $5 billion for highway construction. We complain endlessly about money, yet we will spend as high as $12,000 to keep one child in a jail cell for one year when most could be helped far better in small group homes for a third of that sum.

We know our juvenile prisons are failures, yet we plan to increase their capacities by almost fifty percent. We deplore the need to put non-delinquents together with hard core child criminals—and some 10,000 in with adult prisoners—yet unblushingly continue to do it. In 1961, New York State passed a law forbidding non-delinquents to be placed in facilities housing delinquents. The jails started to empty. Suddenly there was no need for all those guards. Forty per cent were let go. They protested. The legislators repealed the law and returned to the old system.

Few people feel any sense of outrage. I met in Chicago with a group of lawyers and judges who spend their days working with children in court. They impressed me as decent men and women. They uttered all the right words. But they spoke with a curious hollowness of feeling. As the evening wore on, I found myself being grateful that the future of my children did not depend on their concern.

"The way things are now, it is probably better for everyone if young delinquents are not detected," says the former director of the New York State Division for Youth. "Too many of them get worse in our care." Not one state in the country, adds the National Council on Crime and Delinquency, is doing a proper job of rehabilitating children in trouble.

We are a slipshod people. We tend to do nothing unless a crisis is at hand, and then we seek simplistic, temporary measures. We wrap ourselves in our comforts, tend to think the universe is where we are and blink at those who are cold, hungry, sick, in trouble. But the time of slippage may be ending. The time may be beginning when, compassion and purity of purpose aside, *we* are going to be hurt signigicantly if we don't reach out to those "aliens" who dare not to be self sufficient. "If you are among brigands and you are silent, you are a brigand yourself," a folk saying goes. Civilization is not a matter of museums and global communication. It derives from a quality of mind and of concern. And by that definition, we, of course, are not a civilized nation at all, rather a self-centered, stupid one.

"It is undignified," psychiatrist Benjamin Pasamanick said bitterly a few years ago, "for a professional to scream in the streets. 'You would lose your effectiveness,' said my colleagues. 'You would lose your place at the table,' said the inner voices."

Not enough as yet are screaming in the streets.

The emperor is naked where treatment of delinquent–troubled–children in this country is concerned. And if the professionals in all disciplines, *those who know,* don't point at the exposure, who will?

by
Charles Mangel

Making the Case for Behavior as an Expression of Physiological Condition

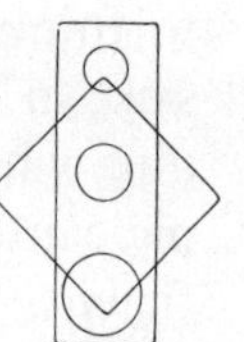

I am very fortunate that my two careers have complemented one another. On the one hand, my medical training has enabled me to identify organic or functional abnormalities among youngsters who have come before me in court. On the other hand, my judicial experience has given me insight into the mischief potential of children brought into my medical office. It has been a great satisfaction to help rehabilitate children in two ways.

I believe strongly that disruptive behavior, everything from truancy to shoplifting, which brings youngsters into juvenile courts often results from medical difficulties of which both the parents and the authorities are unaware. At least 25 percent of our delinquency can be blamed on organic reasons.

I remember Lillian, a sixteen year old, who was arrested for stealing a car. Only a few months before she had been charged with shoplifting at a neighborhood department store. I ordered a complete physical work-up on Lillian and the results showed that she was suffering from a physical disorder known as hyperinsulinism.

Her pancreas was secreting too much insulin, and this was driving her blood sugar down. Now, when your blood sugar is too low, you're going to feel restless, jumpy, fidgety. Your central nervous system is likely to be affected, and your emotional stability can go haywire. Because you're unable to think rationally, you may be unable to act rationally.

This is what happened to Lillian. Her organic difficulty was causing her to act in an antisocial way. Her behavior problem was just the result of her organic problem. A combination of proper medication, guidance, and a carefully prescribed diet–high fat, low carbohydrates, normal protein–soon corrected the difficulty.

I also remember Charlie, twelve years old, who was charged with chronic truancy. He was a very rude youngster who wouldn't listen to anyone, not even the judge. His father kept insisting that all the boy needed was a good thrashing. But I learned that he'd already been beaten more times than he could count and I vetoed more of the same treatment. I had a hunch about this boy because he spoke in a very loud voice. I asked questions like: where does he sit when he watches television, and how loud does he turn it on? Then I ordered a hearing test. It turned out that Charlie had a 50 percent hearing impairment–more than enough to cause him to be inattentive at school and at home. This is why he became frustrated and played hooky. We explained the situation to his parents and his teachers, got him a hearing aid, and his truancy days were over.

Hearing and visual function and perception are generally taken for granted. This is a mistake. The child who doesn't hear or see well is bound to become frustrated and exhibit behavioral symptoms. And don't count too much on the Snellen chart. All it tells you is the child's ability to recognize letters at twenty feet, and there is so much more to vision than that!

Let me give you one more case history. A seventeen year old girl, who was hyperactive, unmanageable, and sexually delinquent, was brought to my court. Her parents, good people, were half out of their minds with worry and despair. When the girl confronted me in court, she complained of feelings of suffocation and appeared very agitated. I ordered an electrocardiogram and discovered that she had an atrial flutter (irregular heartbeat). Further examination and an iodine scan revealed that her thyroid gland was not functioning properly. These organic difficulties were clearly responsible for her behavior. What she needed was medical treatment, not punishment.

In my medical practice, I found many children in whom I could detect signs of future delinquent behavior. Often, when these kids were brought in for minor ailments, the parents would drop hints that made me suspect trouble to come, such as school problems, temper tantrums, etc. These were clues to problems other than those for which the child had been brought in for treatment.

I remember examining one nine year old boy for a common virus infection. I couldn't help noticing how nervous and irritable the child was. When I mentioned this to the mother, she admitted that he was having trouble in school, wouldn't study, and refused to obey his teachers. She told me that he wouldn't listen to reason, that he smashed things, picked fights with other children, and that he slept very poorly.

When I heard this, I gave the boy a far more extensive medical examination than is necessary just to treat a common virus infection. It turned out that he had an abnormal brain wave pattern, determined by an EEG, and this was due to a severe metabolic problem.

You see, metabolism is the process by which energy is made available for all bodily functions—everything from respiration to glandular activity. A disturbance of the metabolism could affect the intellect and the emotions, and the functioning of the brain itself. This is what happened here, and it was no wonder that the child wouldn't listen to reason. No amount of reasoning in the world could reach him until his metabolism is stabilized.

I am on the School Board in Dade County, and we are now focusing on screening tests for early recognition of learning disabilities. Before my term expires next year, I hope to see money budgeted so that any child who cannot perform as the teacher or the parents expect him to perform can have a thorough medical evaluation. We are hoping for six hospital beds for the early recognition child where we can do an EEG, the sugar tolerance test, some allergy studies, a complete profile. In this way perhaps we can prevent the kind of case I saw recently in which a mother was hauled into court because her child kept falling asleep in class. Come to find out he was allergic to an antihistamine which he had been taking for a stuffed-up nose! We decided it was better for him to suffer with a stuffy nose than to sleep all day. Judges must get in the habit of making sure of medical work-ups and facts before pronouncing judgment.

I feel sure that in ten years all psychotic and related disorders will be cured through chemistry, as now evidenced in treatment of manic-depressives and schizophrenics. You Texas people should check Lubbock where the lithium content of the water is high and there is less aggressiveness and disorder there, statistically, than in any other city! I am convinced that there are chemical and medical reasons for learning disabilities and behavioral problems, and I think, as judges, we must make very sure before we pronounce.

Grateful appreciation is extended to Today's Health for permission to include in this paper excerpts from "Delinquents are His Patients" by Arthur Henley which appeared in the November, 1969, issue.

by
Ben J. Sheppard

Other Psychological and Social Problems of Learning Disabled Youth

Recently I was invited to tour an institution for the mentally retarded. Along the way a young man about twenty two years old intruded upon our company and said to me, "Hey, you! What's your name?" I didn't say anything. I ignored him and continued on my way. My hosts tried to shoo him away, but he was not shoo-awayable, and he intruded again into the audience. He looked at me and said, "Hey, you! Are you married?" Again I didn't respond, and, of course, my guides were very upset because they thought they had invited an expert on mental retardation, and he wasn't even nice to the mentally retarded. They tried to shoo him away once more, but still he was not shoo-awayable and again intruded, saying directly to me, "Hey, you! I want to know your name." Then I looked at him, and I said, "Sir, I don't know who you are, and I don't have to talk to you." He regarded me for a moment and said, "Hmm, you have a point. I'm sorry to intrude in this way but I was curious to find out who you were, and I wanted to talk to you." It was my finest teaching moment because we sat down and for twenty minutes had an intelligent conversation. The people in the institutions were astonished because until that time they had not realized that this young man was not mentally retarded but was, indeed, learning disabled.

I didn't need a fancy psychological examination. I didn't need medical studies, or anything except the opportunity to talk to him in a manner that suggested I respected him. The way we treat people is the way they are going to respond to us!

We have an extraordinary situation in this country. We are not educating ten percent of the population, and the cost of this equals the cost of the education of the other ninety percent. We pay an enormous price. Every index of psychopathology correlates with poor school experiences. We have a dilemma of enormous proportion, and remediation is a national scandal. Every large city in this country is reporting a reduction of reading and arithmetic scores despite compensatory education, and we are still compensatorying all over the place! A kid hates to read for five minutes—we give it to him for an hour and a half! A kid can't stand arithmetic for five minutes—we remediate him for two and a half hours! I want you to pass a rumor: we must not try to unblock a block with a block.

We had better concern ourselves with the psychological dimensions of people in trouble. We had better understand that a lot of our young people may be hyperactive, they may have short attention spans and they may not be able to handle anything that's concrete. They may not be able to deal with anything that isn't relevant, but I say it is curious that the way we have described the brain injured is the same way we have described the blacks, the Puerto Ricans, the disadvantaged and the emotionally disturbed.

A lot of the young people who have a short attention span in a school situation, play a pinball machine or Monopoly for hours. Where is the short attention span? Where is the hyperactivity? Some are hyperactive and need medication but many are hyperactive and have a short attention span in response to inappropriate situations. We hear so much about this notion of perseveration. Some of you think you know what perseveration is: repeating things over and over and over again. But that's not what it is: it's being a pain in the ass! A kid says–and you have seen it in your classrooms–"Did I do right? Did I do all right? Am I doing good?" The teacher concludes that this is perseveration due to brain damage, so what happens is, "Oh, yes, honey, you are doing all right, you are doing okay, you are doing fine." Of course, this response is reinforcing the inappropriate behavior. Instead, just say to the kid, "Listen, the next time you ask for praise, I won't give it to you even if you deserve it because you keep asking over and over again." And the kid will say, "I do not. I do not. I do not." Do you know what will happen if you don't give him praise when he asks for it? In two weeks' time the behavior is extinguished. Of course, he may find something else to annoy you with, but, at least, it won't be asking for praise.

And what about relevance? The whole curriculum has become relevant. Dick and Jane are black and urban and, of course, Spot remains integrated, yet I suspect not a single black or Puerto Rican or learning disabled child had learned to read as a result. Relevance is boring! Have you ever noticed that? Take Dr. Seuss–he's completely irrelevant! He makes up his own words and his own fantasies, and everybody likes Dr. Seuss. You watch Sesame Street (you say you watch it because you want to know what your kids are into, but you like it yourselves) and why do you like it? Because Sesame Street is irrelevant! The garbage can talks to the big bird! We have to do some things that are relevant but, for heaven's sake, let's acknowledge that whatever is relevant in our lives is usually boring.

We need to remediate some people. Some people need drugs, and some people need some kind of walking rails and perceptual training, but in my experience, the people who are not learning are not learning mainly for psychological reasons. Do the medical studies–sure! Let's have medication–sure! But eighty percent of our people who are not learning are not learning for psychological reasons. They enter school, and they already know how to read "pizza," "Howard Johnson," and a few obscenities, and we can't teach them how to read "the" and "but." What is this? Illiterates all over the world have been taught to read as adults, yet we can't teach kids how to read. We can't teach them how to read because we haven't understood their psychological dimensions. If a kid feels he can't read, and he hates to read, and he feels he's no good because he's being tested at reading, we give him *reading*. Don't unblock a block with a block! Because we have not understood, we have created so many disturbances in young people. Now we need to retreat a little bit, cool it a little bit, say to hell with the curriculum (if you don't have "tenure," however, don't "listen" to anything I have to say).

What counts with handicapped young people, whether they are delinquent and/or learning disabled, is how they feel about themselves, their socialization skills and whether or not they have friends. If I had only one yardstick to use, I would measure loneliness and boredom. We must begin to help people understand that if they are bored, they are also boring. We have to elevate the spirit of these young people in trouble. We have to teach them something new. We have to help them achieve a sense of ego, a sense of socialization, a sense of making friends. How many of you get depressed every now and then? The rest of you are lying! Let's try again–how many of you get depressed once in a while? The rest of you are in deep trouble! I'm going to tell you exactly what to do the next time you get depressed so you will understand what so many of these young people need. First, I want you to go the refrigerator. (Of course, most of you do that anyway.) Get something sweet like a Coke. You will notice that if you drink a Coke, you feel better for about two and a half minutes. The blood sugar level has risen but now you don't know what to do with that two and a half minutes–so you have to have another Coke and another Coke and . . . Take only one Coke, and now you have two and a half minutes to learn something new. Call up a friend on the telephone and say, "What's new?" If they say, "Nothing," hang up right away and call up someone else! Look up a new word in the dictionary, read an article about something you know little about, and you will elevate your spirits and feel better. That's what we have to do with our children in trouble. Teach them something new. Instead of opening up a window and exercising which makes kids even more tired, every teacher should have a repertoire of one hundred irrelevant, five-minute lessons. Teach kids astrological signs, capitols of countries they have never heard of, magic tricks, something exciting, which will elevate the spirit.

Every high school in this country has at least one hundred disruptive, difficult kids who are not learning, who are not achieving. It's not that teachers don't want to teach them; I've been a teacher, and most teachers want to teach. Anyone who has been a teacher knows that the process of not teaching is exhausting, and it is the one or two children in the classroom whom they are not teaching who make them so tired. And, of course, the children who are not learning are exhausted, too, by the process. I hope you will remember that if a child is not learning anything during the school day, you should assign a nap. Assign homework only to children who are achieving because achieving and learning are stimulating, are exciting, and they are ready for homework.

And so we need to teach people new things. I suggest that we get them out of the schools for awhile. Let's apprentice them to a retired artist in the community, to a retired Olympic swimmer, a cabinet maker, someone who is dying to teach young people something new. Elevate their spirit, teach them to bowl, teach them chess, or scrabble, card games. Get them out so that their egos can be enhanced, and then perhaps they will want to learn "academic" subjects. The psychological reward of learning something new is a feeling of accomplishment, a feeling that life can be worthwhile. Sure, you may need medical treatment. Sure, you need studies and some discipline, but unless we understand that we need to balance these things with excitement, our students will continue to turn us off.

I suggested this apprenticeship approach in a school, and the teachers were excited about the plan, and the students were excited about the plan, and the parents were excited about the plan, but the superintendent vetoed it because he couldn't figure out a way of keeping attendance!

And now the missing dimension of this whole piece: sex! We have to understand that the *more* a person knows about his or her sexuality, the more responsible they are in their sexual behavior. Don't listen to people who say that the less people know about sex, the better off they are. The opposite is true! The birthrate is going down in every age group except among teenagers. Last year almost a million teenagers became pregnant. There were three million new cases of venereal disease in this country, half of them among young people. We need to help our young people understand something about their sexuality, and if we don't help them understand it, they will express it in sexual irresponsibility, in delinquency, and other forms of aggressive behavior.

In recent studies, we learned that half of all the young people in a high school thought the only time a girl could become pregnant was to have sex during her menstrual period, so they carefully avoided the menstrual period. In one school in which there were three hundred girls who were pregnant, we asked the young people why they didn't use birth control measures, and they replied, "Oh, we did. We took one of our mother's pills." Or "We didn't think we could become pregnant if we had sex standing up." (You can.)

Now let's take something like masturbation. Everybody's into it these days. It's the latest thing. But we must understand and be comfortable with the subject of masturbation ourselves or we can't communicate with the teenagers. Example: the modern mother says to the modern child, "Honey, it's okay, it's normal, it's a part of a normal developmental stage," and then she pauses and says, "If you don't do it too much." And nobody in the United States knows how much is too much! Once a year? Twice a week? After every meal? How much is too much? Even the medical literature says that masturbation is a normal developmental stage but that those who do it too much are shy, retiring, narcissistic, and have no friends. How long does it take to masturbate? Why should it interfere with friends? Some of my best friends are masturbators, and some people I know who have never masturbated have no friends. What's the connection? Masturbation is a normal expression of sexuality and we as adults have no right to interfere with it. Not in the jails, in the institutions, nor in the homes. It has to be private as every sexual act has to be private. And once is too much if you don't enjoy it. If masturbation is an expression of sexuality, then it is a part of growing up and of life itself. Yet people continue to say things like, "Oh, they won't know the real thing. They won't appreciate sex with another person." I reply "Not every meal is a gourmet meal!"

In conclusion, I want to reemphasize that most of the young people we have to worry about are depressed and feel badly about themselves. I say that they must experience a new way of looking at themselves. I say that first and foremost, we have to help them communicate with themselves. Life is not just a meaning, an ethereal meaning that they have to search for. Life is made up of a lot of alternatives, and there are many new and exciting experiences in it that young people can appreciate and understand. Ladies and gentlemen, don't unblock a block with a block!

by
Sol Gordon

This Side of the Court

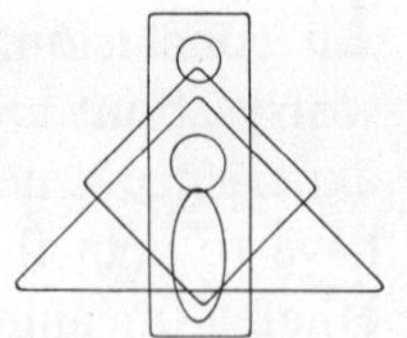

Today in the United States more than eight million children of average to superior intelligence have a learning disability. A strong possibility exists that a large percentage of these children will be referred to the juvenile justice system for such horrendous offenses as truancy, running away, acting out behavior in the classroom or home. Such offenses are common only to children and cease legally to be an offense when an individual reaches the age of majority.

When a learning disabled child is referred to a probation officer, we usually have several options which we may elect to exercise. We may dismiss the matter at intake level; we may place the child on informal probation; or we may incarcerate him with delinquents, thereby bringing him into the juvenile justice system. If we elect the latter procedure, we reinforce his negative behavior, and if we repeat this procedure a sufficient number of times, we most likely will shape this child into a fairly good delinquent.

Frequently, children with a learning disability are not readily accepted by their peer group and may have, over the years, been referred to as "stupid" or "mentally retarded." However, when we lock these children up with delinquents, the delinquents view them primarily as non-conformist and may accept them. In turn, the learning disabled child happily and willingly becomes a follower of any member of a peer group who grants acceptance. Once out of the detention facility, the learning disabled youth will continue an association with delinquent friends and will frequently engage in actual delinquent behavior, such as theft or burglary, if that is the price he must pay for acceptance.

Another course a probation officer may take when he encounters a child with a learning disability is to assume automatically that he is mentally retarded, or that he is not only mentally retarded but also has emotional problems. Teenagers with learning disabilities will have developed emotional problems simply because they have faced failure and frustration day after day in the classroom and have fallen below their parents' expectations at home. In order to gain some insight into what these children are facing, imagine what it would be like to be required to go to a particular job assignment every day and know that you will face nothing but failure and frustration. (If there are any probation officers in the audience, I am certain they can feel empathy with the learning disabled child!)

The Sonoma County Probation Department first became aware of learning disabilities in 1966 through a chance encounter with an obviously intelligent, slightly hyper-verbal, ten-year-old child. We later found out that this child had been irrevocably expelled from a neighboring county's school system and that, as far as they were concerned, his school experience was terminated at the age of ten.

This child was enrolled in a specialized learning center, was receiving prescriptive teaching and progressing exceptionally well.

This was an unnerving experience for me, for I immediately recognized that it was possible that we had been punishing children for years for a condition over which they had no control. As we investigated the matter further, the decision was made to screen a small, specialized caseload of heavily delinquent-oriented children. This initial screening was accomplished by contacting the schools and requesting that they furnish us with each child's grade level and reading level. Of the sixty cases reviewed, the schools had records on fifty. Only ten children (or twenty percent) were reading at grade level. Eighty percent were significantly retarded in reading.

We felt that this was sufficient evidence to explore this matter in greater depth. With the assistance of the Guidance Department of our county school system and through specialized training at a learning center, we eventually developed a screening test which would aid in identifying many different types of learning disabilities. Our test is rather lengthy and detailed, and a much briefer version could be developed. It is a matter of great interest to us that over the years we have noticed a wide span of performance, particularly in the area of dominance. Someday we hope to be able to determine scientifically what significance mixed dominance has as a factor in learning disabilities.

The screening test is administered by two persons, one who gives directions and the other who notes the child's reactions to the directions. Observation is undoubtedly one of the most important aspects of the screening process. It is important that the persons who administer the test put the minor at his ease and are friendly and outgoing. Some standardized tests are used which I will review later. I think it important to note that our test can be administered by anyone who can speak and count. It is also important to point out that we are not making a diagnosis but are developing a write-up for referral purposes.

If the mother is available for interview, we question her regarding her pregnancy. We are particularly interested in any illnesses during pregnancy, in premature bleeding, if the pregnancy was short or normal term, in the birth process (if labor was prolonged or rapid and if instruments were used). We are also interested in learning if the child had any difficulty in breathing or other problems at birth. We attempt to cover all childhood diseases, especially those involving high temperature for an extended period of time, diarrhea, or anything else that might result in dehydration. We also inquire about accidents, especially those involving blows to the head. A primary problem in this area is that frequently parents are not available or they are unable to recall any specific problem or associate a particular disease with a particular child. This interview is not held in the child's presence.

When we move the child into the screening situation, we advise him that we will be asking him to perform a number of different tasks, that we are not interested in *how well* he does them but simply *how* he does them, and that there is no pass/fail involved. We then ask him the name he prefers, his birthdate, the school he attends, grade, favorite teacher, and how well he likes school. These and other general questions are designed to put the child at ease.

We begin our screening in the area of motor coordination, advising the child that he will be standing up and sitting down a number of times during the screening process. We ask him to stand on one foot, noting not only foot preference but also how his body adjusts and if he can balance properly. We then ask him to stand on the unchosen foot, again checking performance to determine how well he is oriented in space. We ask him to hop on one foot, then the other, and to walk backwards. In all of these exercises, we are looking for dominance as well as balance, and, in the last instance, his sense of backspace. We ask him to fold his arms across his chest; the dominant arm will be on top. When clasping hands together, the dominant thumb will be on top. We hand him a coat and ask him to put it on, noting that the subdominant arm will be the first arm inserted in the sleeve. We also administer the Schilder Arm Extension Test.

In fine motor, he is asked to tie his shoes and to bring his pointing fingers together with his eyes closed. We then direct him to sit down, and a pencil is placed in front of him in the middle of a piece of paper. He is asked to organize the paper because information will be dictated. He is asked to write the word "Dictation," and if he balks, we advise him that it doesn't make any difference how he spells it. We further ask that he not erase if he should make an error but simply correct the error beside the word. Other instructions are included in this portion of the screening, but what we are actually attempting to do is determine sidedness or dominance and also to note if he can use both hands in conjunction with each other, how he handles his pencil, and how difficult it is for him to write. We then use the Leavell Test, which also shows preference or sidedness and which indicates whether a child can operate horizontally or only vertically.

We then check for eye preference by having the minor look through a rolled piece of paper. Before giving him the rolled piece of paper, we attempt to distract his attention by suggesting that we want him to look through the paper and tell us which end of the pencil is up, the point or the eraser. We then check visual stability by asking the minor to track the eraser of a pencil horizontally, vertically, and circularly in order to assess his tracking abilities. Convergence is also checked. The standard Peabody Picture Vocabulary Test is administered to determine I.Q. We check visual discrimination by asking the minor to copy a list of simple words, some of which are commonly reversed. To obtain reading level, we use the Wide Range Achievement Test, on which we can spot many sequential problems, and the Gray Oral Reading Test. For auditory discrimination, the Wepman Auditory Discrimination Test and a group of words adapted from the Slingerland Screening Test are used. Dictation paragraphs range from third to eighth grade level, but we usually start with a third grade paragraph. We check the child's sense of directionality by asking him to turn to his right, lift his left arm, touch his left ear with the right hand, touch his right toe with his left hand. We present him with a list of five numbers and ask him to indicate the first number, the middle number, and the next to the last number. We then request that he write the numbers one through ten. We are looking for reversals and improper sequence.

In the area of body image, we ask the child to draw a picture of himself. Many children balk at this, but when they are assured that we don't expect them to be great artists, we usually get their cooperation. This part of the screening is specifically for referral purposes only. (We do not attempt to diagnose.) We then check the child's sense of rhythm by simply tapping out patterns and seeing if he can match them or reproduce them. The final portion of the screening involves number recall with a dictated series of numbers involving three digits, four digits and, finally, five digits. The child is asked to recite the numbers forwards, and then a similar series is dictated, and he is asked to repeat them in reverse. One extremely difficult series that few children have been able to repeat forwards and in reverse is 4, 7, 6, 3, 7.

The entire screening test is then written up and sent to a referral source: a neurologist, a pediatrician, or a school if it has a program for the educationally handicapped.

One of the first boys we screened was Jim, a fifteen year old, who had failed to begin the school year at the start of the ninth grade. The screening revealed that Jim had an I.Q. of 96, was reading at the fourth month level of kindergarten, was unable to write, and had totally opposite reactions in identifying the right or left sides of his body. Although Jim's mother was cooperative, the father would never talk with the probation officer, even on the telephone. We requested that the mother take Jim to a pediatrician, who diagnosed visual perception problems and who also requested that he not be required to take physical education. We visited the school and showed the principal and the vice principal how Jim was performing and further advised them of the pediatrician's name and his recommendations. At that time the school had no program for children with learning disabilities, so we simply requested that they remove all pressure and not force him to take physical education.

When the probation officer took Jim to school the next day, the first question was, "Where are your gym clothes? Don't think you are going to pull that same old stuff this year!" Jim phoned that evening and reported that in his first class the teacher gave him a form to fill out; in his second class he was called upon to do arithmetic at the blackboard. Through a lack of communication, this school system completely destroyed Jim in one day.

Jim eventually finished his school career at the age of eighteen when he left the continuation high school (a school for problem children, especially drug users) in the tenth grade. He obtained a job as a dishwasher in a pancake house and was told to go in the back room and bring out a can of strawberry syrup. He spent half an hour attempting to find out how to pick out the right can. This experience cost him his job. He later got a trial job helping to clean up the kitchen of another restaurant with a promise of future employment. However, after cleaning up the kitchen, when he returned for his job, he was advised that someone else had been hired. His third and final job was working for half pay from midnight to 8:00 AM. in a rest home that cared for a number of elderly patients. His job was to check each patient every fifteen minutes and change the bedding and clothing as required. After three nights of work, he resigned. He is now twenty two years old and has been declared totally and permanently disabled for life, receiving Aid to the Totally Disabled in the amount of $140 per month. Jim never committed any delinquent act, and I think part of this can be attributed to the fact that we did not involve him in the juvenile justice system with its systematic incarcerations. If the $140 a month that Jim is currently receiving had been applied toward a good prescriptive teaching program in his early years, he might very well be a productive citizen today.

Several years ago I stopped in at Juvenile Hall on a Saturday and noted that a twelve year old boy had been admitted to the Hall as a runaway from school. When I spoke with him, the first question I asked was, "Why do you run away from school?" His answer was, "Because I'm stupid and ugly." He was neither. He was an attractive youngster with an I.Q. of 104. However, the screening test revealed that he was reading at the fifth month level of first grade, had visual perceptual problems, including poor visual memory, sequential problems, omission of letter parts and rotation of letters. His dictated work indicated an inability to link up the acoustical properties of a word with its lexical percepts, although the Wepman Auditory Discrimination Test did not indicate a serious problem in this area. This young man was put on probation and placed in an educationally handicapped class. He successfully completed probation and has not been referred back to our department. He will soon attain the age of eighteen years.

A final case history involves a fifteen year old youth who was in tenth grade and enrolled in slow classes. He was failing all courses and had been expelled from one class. However, he had not formally been referred to the Probation Department. His mother brought him in for a screening, a service we provide to the public as a delinquency prevention method. This young man had an extremely poor attitude at home and in school but cooperated well in the screening test. He was found to have an I.Q. of 127, was reading at the fifth month level of a college freshman but was dysgraphic. The minor and his mother were referred to a neurologist who has a child study center whose staff included a remedial teacher who worked with the youngster on his handwriting. He completed the school year with A's and B's and continues to earn A's and B's this year. His self image and attitude at home have shown definite improvement.

Up to this point we have been discussing diverting children who have delinquent tendencies from the juvenile justice system. It is evident that all children with learning disabilities who come to the attention of Probation Departments for criminal offenses cannot be diverted and will have to be processed through the courts. What can be done for these children? First, I think it is necessary to establish the fact that a disproportionate number of children with learning disabilities are entering the juvenile justice system. In 1969, the Department of Health, Education and Welfare published a study entitled "Reading Disorders in the United States." On page 29 of that report is the following statement: "Studies indicate that 75 percent of juvenile delinquents are significantly retarded in reading." It is further indicated that in 1968 the cost for detaining a juvenile delinquent in a federal institution was $6,935 per year. I would assume that that cost has risen considerably since that date.

The Sonoma County Probation Department is presently seeking a joint grant proposal with Stanford Research Institute. The first year of the project will cover seven basic phases or tasks.

Task 1 will consist of a review and revision of diagnostic procedures for specific learning disabilities currently used by the Sonoma County Probation Department.

Task 2 involves the development of a brief screening device for specific learning disabilities. This screening device can be administered in approximately ten minutes and will give an indication of those children who should be screened in depth.

Task 3 will involve an inventory of resources (e.g., financial support, professional competence) and limitations or constraints (e.g., attitudes toward inter-agency cooperation) in or near Sonoma County to be considered in developing a diagnostic and remediation system for learning disabilities for the Sonoma County Probation Department.

Task 4 will involve screening approximately 2,000 Sonoma County students for specific learning disabilities and surveying approximately 500 teachers concerning the incidence of learning disabilities in students.

Task 5 will involve a comparison of the incidence of learning disabilities among juvenile referrals to the Sonoma County Probation Department with the incidence of learning disabilities among Sonoma County students and California Youth Authority wards in the same age range.

Task 6 will involve the development of a diagnostic and remediation system for juvenile referrals to the Sonoma County Probation Department with specific learning disabilities.

Task 7 will involve the preparation of a detailed status report summarizing the first year's activities, together with policy implications and recommendations.

Although previous studies have been made regarding the correlation between learning disabilities and delinquency, if this grant proposal is funded, more than 4,000 children who are referred for delinquent tendencies and delinquency will be screened. We will also have the advantage of scientific validation of our studies by the Stanford Research Institute, which has an international reputation for professional competence.

The study will doubtless dramatically point up the need for early identification and treatment of children with learning disabilities as well as the necessity for remedial programs for those who are already in the system. If those two programs can be developed, we will not only prevent a large number of children from entering the juvenile justice system but will also assist those presently in the system to achieve success in learning and will be able to reduce the present frightening rate of recidivism.

Such programs will unquestionably prevent a huge amount of human suffering, will save the taxpayers a tremendous amount of money through developing productive citizens, and, most important, will keep a considerable number of children on this side of the law.

by
William Mulligan

Delinquents are Disabled

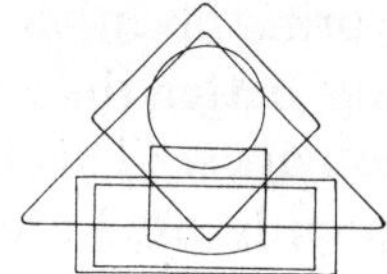

My experience with adolescent delinquents has been a frustrating thing, because I have become convinced that most of these young people feel miserable about themselves. They hate themselves, have given up hope that anyone cares about them, and they make me feel miserable because I realize how much we have failed to be able to help them. I have joined the ranks of the many frustrated professionals who have attempted to become involved in the rehabilitation and improvement of the quality of life of young people we call delinquent. Two statistics in particular have been most discouraging. The first is that recidivism rates among delinquents have climbed to a rate hovering around 85 percent. This is not a drastic increase from what has existed previously, but the rate has not declined and has even escalated somewhat from that reported ten years ago. Secondly, the average age for first incarceration for delinquents is now below age thirteen years for the first time, and this age is decreasing yearly. That means, that chances are strong that delinquents will be labelled by age twelve or thirteen and will most likely remain so for the rest of their lives.

These numbers are stark testimony to the fact that, despite all the best efforts of judges, mental health and rehabilitation professionals, there has still been no systematic success in the fight against the waste of young lives. It seems to me after seventy years of trying the best methods known to psychology, psychiatry and other areas of rehabilitation–after seventy years of utter failure and the waste of thousands of young lives–we ought to think about the possibility that we may have been approaching the problem the wrong way. Even a rat learns that after banging his head on the door he ought to try a different one.

Aside from a few exceptions, traditionally rehabilitation for juvenile offenders has taken two general routes. There is the "work 'em hard" technique which emphasizes discipline, custody and the allegedly remedial effects of sweat. This method has advantages in allowing society to wreak vengeance upon these so-called criminals, and also is well known for the brutality and aggressiveness of reformatory personnel. After all, if the attendants and guards could not express their sadistic tendencies on these wastrels, think of how much more crime there might be on the streets. The second approach has been more treatment oriented–a descendent of our psycho-dynamic heritage: the assumption is that delinquency is a form of psychopathology like neurosis or psychosis, and that the best way to rehabilitate the youngster is to provide different forms of psychotherapeutic activities within the institution.

Both of these methods have certain logical appeal to them and there is much support for their use by intelligent and learned advocates. Nevertheless, neither has worked. Neither type of approach has been able to produce results that have been any better than simply allowing the youngsters to vegetate in cells or meaningless activities. (This latter "treatment" technique, I might add, is still the most frequently used around the country.)

I would like to present the results of some research today that cries for a wholesale change in our attitudes toward, and treatment of, young people whom we've been calling delinquent. I am a believer that the label you pin on someone has a lot to do with how that person gets treated, so I am first of all going to stop calling these children delinquent (which is a social term), and begin using the label "disabled"–since that more accurately describes their condition. They are disabled youngsters who have been imprisoned, forgotten, ignored, stripped of self-esteem and have been the targets of social vindictiveness and hypocrisy. I have evidence that most delinquents are disabled, and have been disabled since early childhood, possibly since birth. The fact that their disabilities have been incorrectly diagnosed and that their lives have been wasted because they've been called delinquent, is, in my mind, one of the most horrendous failures of the legal, medical, educational, and psychological professions.

Our project began in 1970 with a grant from the Rhode Island Governor's Commission on Crime and Delinquency, from money distributed by the U.S. Department of Justice, LEAA. The grant and project is now in its fifth year of renewal. Although the project has both diagnostic and treatment components, I will spend my time here describing the diagnostic aspects. The diagnostic element consists of the following procedures, which have been done on a random population of new admissions to the R.I. Training School for Boys.

Each boy is interviewed for approximately one hour, during which a detailed history is gathered. The information is later checked against whatever can be retrieved from court records. After the clinical interview, the complete Halstead-Reitan Neuropsychology Battery is administered, including the Wechsler Intelligence Scales, the Wide Range Achievement Tests, several personality measurements, as well as all the tests for specific impairment. The complete procedure takes from one full day to one and a half days per child, exclusive of time required for scoring and interpretation. The diagnostic procedures are carried out by one of several research assistants who have been specifically trained for their parts of the evaluation. All interpretations are done personally by me in consultation with at least one of the research assistants.

The data we have is summarized in many ways. The larger number (second column on the table) is data taken for all youngsters we've seen, regardless of randomness or other experimental sampling considerations. Once methodological concerns are exercised, many youngsters were excluded from the experimental sample due to factors which might confound interpretation. The selected sample, then, is in the first column. Which figures you use depend on your purposes. If you are interested in looking at the total picture, regardless of making hypotheses about causation, then the second column is more appropriate.

Table 1

Specific Disabilities Found in 46 Selected, and 122 Non-Selected, Adolescent Delinquents

DISABILITY	NUMBER OF TIMES OCCURRING	
	N = 46	N = 22
Visual-perceptual or visual-motor disability	14	67 (55%)
Perceptual-motor disability other than visual	8	38 (31%)
Impaired nonverbal concept formation	12	37 (31%)
Auditory discrimination or memory disability	8	35 (30%)
Impaired kinesthetic feedback	14	31 (28%)
Nonspecific dyslexic disorder	4	18
Arithmetic reasoning	3	11
Total number showing at least one major disability	26 (56%)	86 (70%)

These data are sobering. Seventy percent of the youngsters being imprisoned in the training school had measurable disabilities significant enough to warrant professional attention. Examination results indicate that these disabilities have been chronic—that is, they have existed for some time, perhaps from birth, without having been noticed by anyone associated with the child. We are currently evaluating a control group of youngsters in a city high school who come from similar socioeconomic backgrounds but have not been delinquent. Although final results aren't completed, early data on about one half of the control group indicate that the percentage of disabilities there will run at about 20 percent. It is important to remember that we are not making any statements about etiology or causation of these disabilities. We feel that at this point in the lives of these young people, questions of causality are academic. It is clear that these disabilities exist, that we have failed to find them, and that the resultant effects on the lives of these youngsters have forced them out of the mainstream of society.

These figures certainly don't pretend that every disabled child who doesn't get treated will become delinquent. Nevertheless, after carefully reviewing the case histories of these youngsters, I feel that our project has demonstrated that failure to recognize significant disabilities early in a child's school career sets into motion a devastating series of events that, for a large number of unfortunates, ends up in a reformatory or juvenile court.

The cycle begins with early problems at home. The child was showing perceptual and attentional problems even prior to school, but the behavior was written off as "ornery" or "uncooperative" personality. The child enters the early grades of school already accustomed to the fact that he won't be able to do things as well as expected of him, that he will fail and be humiliated continually. This prophecy is fulfilled in school as teachers, considering the child "a behavior problem," punish and ridicule him for failures or for behaviors that he cannot control. The child begins to think of himself as a loser, as someone who can never hope to live up to what people expect of him. Rather than face the embarrassment of continual failure in front of friends and teachers, the behavioral signs become even more pronounced. Clowning around and general disruptiveness become the ways which best insulate this youngster from having to face continual and repeated failure. He becomes much more successful as a clown or troublemaker than he ever could be as a student. Teachers now are completely diverted away from any learning problems and concentrate solely on how to deal with the child's behavior. He gets further and further behind, becomes more and more of a problem. Eventually he's suspended, drops out or is thrown out of school to roam the streets, and the inevitable road to delinquency is well under way. The original problems have never been dealt with; the child is thought of as incorrigible. His problems are seen as psychogenic, not as the result of deflated self-esteem and fears of inadequacy, all of which have been generated by disability. His prophecy of himself as a loser has been fulfilled.

Once the cycle begins, it is vicious and insidious. Once a child drops out of school the chances are estimated that one in three will appear in juvenile court. Some experts feel that the percentage is even higher. Once a child appears in court it has already been mentioned that 80 percent will be back. What hasn't been mentioned is that, when they return, it will usually be for continually increasing seriousness of offense. While the first offense may be for truancy or breaking and entering, later offenses usually involve assault or the use of dangerous weapons. And we also know that 75 percent of the inmates of most adult prisons began their careers as juvenile offenders. The record is discouraging. It is all the more frustrating since *at no point in this destructive cycle has the basic disability been addressed:* not in school, not in the courts, not in rehabilitation institutions. Teachers, who should be the most logical personnel to discover learning problems, are hopelessly untrained to do so. Judges can't be expected to be able to diagnose disabilities, but even if they could, most correctional institutions wouldn't know what to do with them. The youngsters are treated either as criminals or seriously psychopathological, with no attention directed toward the basic disability.

Judges are particularly vulnerable. Stranded by an educational training system that continues to ignore disability training as preparation for every teacher, some judges have begun to be able to suspect the problem. But there is literally nowhere to turn. Except for very few, institutions and agencies dealing with delinquents have no knowledge about disabilities nor training in how to deal with them. This is a plea for judges and public officers in general to exercise whatever authority they have in demanding three critical changes:

1. Disability detection training should be a mandatory requirement in all teacher training programs, especially for teachers training for grades

kindergarten through three. It is scandalous that teacher training institutions ignore their responsibility here.

2. Early detection diagnostic screening should be required as part of applications for kindergarten and first grade.
3. Installation in reformatories and training schools of diagnostic and remediative facilities for detecting and correcting disabilities.
4. People who work with kids must give a damn about them; instead of degrees and fancy training, they must demonstrate compassion and respect for the dignity of the people they are working with.

Usually the most significant concern about instituting programs such as these is the cost factor. People, legislators, ask "How much will it cost to do these things?" While there will be some necessary initial expenses, I think it might be more appropriate to ask "How much does it cost us *not* to be instituting such programs?" In Rhode Island, according to recent figures, it costs the taxpayers $26,000 per year for *each* youngster in the R.I. Training Schools. Thus, for the average delinquent, who spends three to five years in a reformatory, the cost is around $100,000 *per child.* This figure, though startling, does not include the expenses generated when three-fourths of these kids get older and become adult prisoners. Nor does the financial factor account for the misery and devastation of human potential that current juvenile rehabilitation practices cause in this country.

As people in positions where you can exercise some control over what happens to the lives of youngsters, I urge you to become advocates for these neglected young people. Do whatever is in your power to help institute the kinds of basic changes mentioned as well as make certain that you don't contribute to the destruction of youngsters by condoning outmoded and ineffective institutions which have merely served as junior jails. Instead of sending delinquents to euphemistically named prisons, you should realize that these kids are pathetic, disabled people who have never been successful at anything, who hate themselves for their inadequacies and who need disability remediation, encouragement and compassion in order to have a chance at making their lives useful or satisfying. Dick Compton and Bruce Burt will be describing one model of such a program that has had dramatic success in Colorado. I hope you will do what you can to institute such innovations in your own districts. Don't just sit about and nod in agreement. Do something!

by
Allan Berman

Diagnostic Evaluation of Committed Delinquents

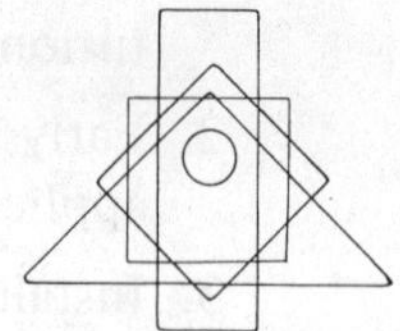

The Division of Youth Services is that Division of the Department of Institutions which handles, by law, the adjudicated and committed delinquents and "Children in Need of Supervision." Within the Division of Youth Services, my office is responsible for planning, coordinating funding and budget control, evaluation and educational personnel within the four institutions and five detention centers of the Division (see Figure 1, next page).

The institutions and detention centers are established by the Colorado Juvenile Code which provides for four treatment institutions:

1. Mount View Girls' School, which is really a misnomer since most of the girls are transported to another institution.
2. Lookout Mountain School for Boys for their educational programs.
3. Two open environment youth camps, Golden Gate Youth Camp, west of Denver, and
4. Lathrop Park Youth Camp in the southern region of the state.

Five detention centers are scattered around the state and are designed as diagnostic receiving centers for various judicial districts. In addition, there are various group homes and alternative placement facilities, some operated by the Division of Youth Services, some privately operated under contract to the Division of Youth Services.

Within these various institutions, the Colorado Juvenile Code provides that we serve:

1. Adjudicated delinquents. These are students aged twelve to nineteen who have been committed by juvenile courts.
2. Children in Need of Supervision (CHINS) who are wards of the court.
3. Detention students who are under temporary restraint or who, after a hearing, are committed to the Department of Institutions and placed in detention centers for diagnosis and evaluation.
4. Juvenile Parole students who have been released from institutions and who may be on parole for a maximum of two years.
5. In addition, we handle some special students such as youth under fifteen committed by federal courts and, by contract, delinquent youth from Alaska.

Figure 1

GOVERNOR
STATE of COLORADO
DEPARTMENT
of INSTITUTIONS
MENTAL
RETARDATION
ADULT
CORRECTIONS
MENTAL
HEALTH
DIVISION of
YOUTH SERVICES
ADMINISTRATION
CHIEF DIVISION of
YOUTH SERVICES
COMMUNITY
SERVICES
EDUCATION
MAINTENANCE
BUSINESS
INSTITUTIONAL
TREATMENT
4
INSTITUTIONS
5
DETENTION
CENTERS

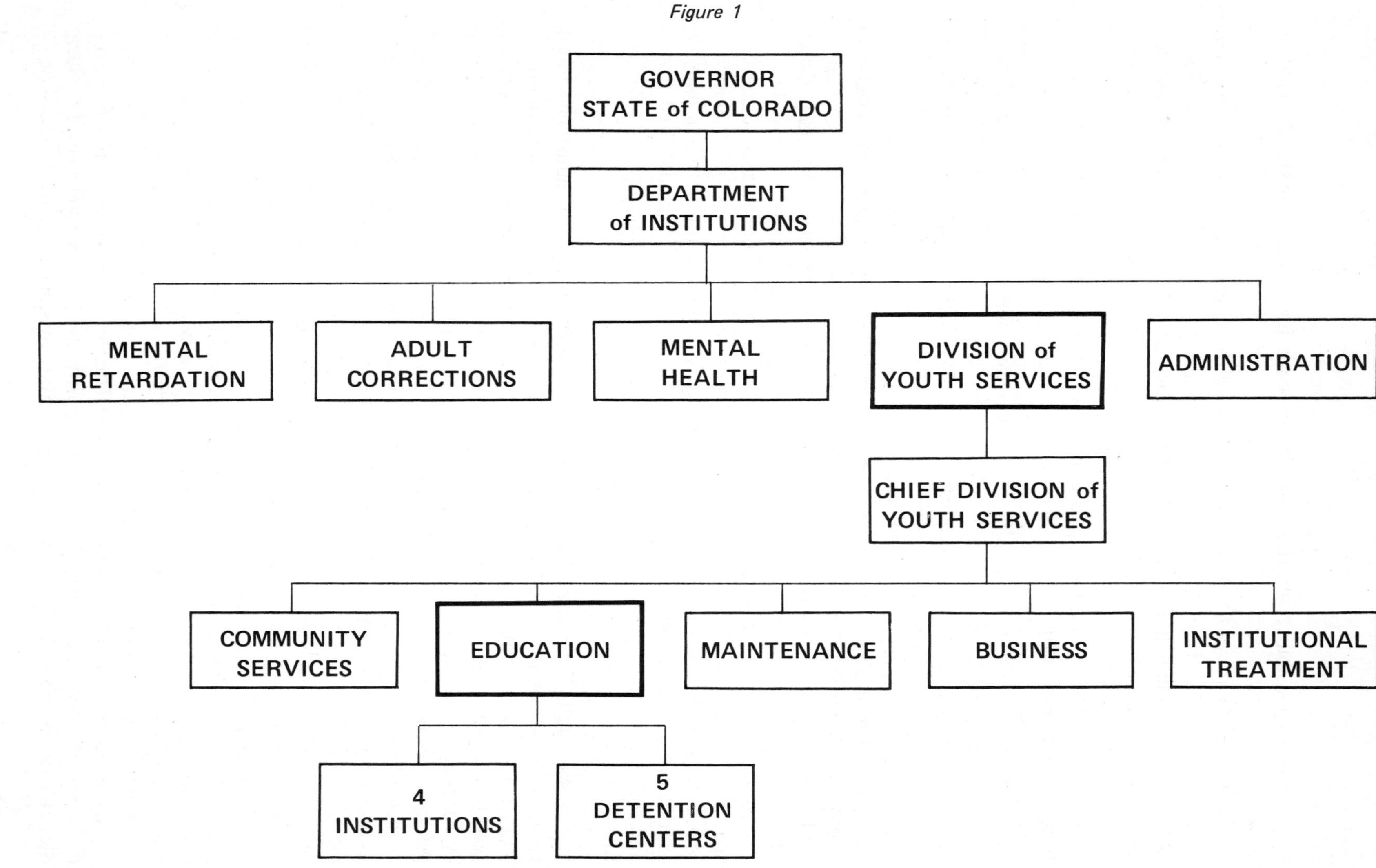

Our responsibility and the scope of our work deals with these students within these institutions.

In 1968, I left an administrative position in the public schools in the Colorado Springs area to join the Division of Youth Services as curriculum coordinator because I saw an opportunity to develop laboratory situations unavailable to public schools for treatment of those youths whom the public schools were failing. One of the first steps was to develop a grant proposal for a diagnostic receiving center which was funded by the Law Enforcement Assistance Administration and which began operation in 1969.

Based upon the first results from this center, plus our previous experience, it became evident that most standardized tests and other diagnostic efforts were designed primarily to measure academic or physical functioning levels *only*. Obviously what was needed was to find out *why* the child was functioning at his level in order to interpret to teachers simply and readily the approaches which were needed to enable a student to build on a functioning level. A good teacher could provide more information about the actual academic functioning level and skill development in twenty minutes than a full day of standardized testing. Observation of physical activities by trained observers were much more effective in determining physical malfunction than were standardized tests. We soon discovered that many well known tests tend to classify everything into terms which are meaningless to most treators and which do not identify a specific problem in a manner that would be convertible to treatment, so we threw out most standardized tests and text books and began developing alternative means of determining causes for low functioning levels.

As results from the diagnostic center became sufficiently numerous to be monitored and compared to prior diagnostic and evaluation records from public schools and other sources, we discovered that a large percentage of those previous evaluations, which generally had been based upon standardized tests administered by itinerant or contracted personnel who saw the student only during the time of testing, were invalid. They had, for example, a large number of students classified as mentally retarded who obviously, on close observation, were not. But if they were not mentally retarded, why were they so far behind? Why did they appear to the itinerant psychologist as mentally retarded if, indeed, they were not? Why were they unable to learn? These were some of the questions to which we resolved to find answers.

Fortunately, at this time two things happened. I became Director of Education, and we found a school psychologist who was very different. She was willing to admit, for example, that she didn't know all the answers and that there could possibly be things not covered within the "ivory tower" which might have some significance. Most important, she considered each child as someone different, not to be compared with all of the other cases. Helen Hursch has kept a firm hand on the diagnostic processes since 1971. More recently she has been aided by Dr. Steve Bloom with the assigned responsibility within the Division of Youth Services of developing a total observational diagnostic program to cover all areas of need. This is a reflection of the new philosophies of treating troubled youth which Jerry Agee, Chief of the Division, began implementing when he assumed that position in 1972.

In 1971, it became obvious that, in addition to developing diagnosis, we also needed to explore in greater depth the treatment process as a follow-up to diagnosis. Lathrop Park Youth Camp was excited about its treatment program and wanted to do more. We made money and consulting services available to them with the aid of Title I ESEA so they could develop additional depth and diagnosis in a more sophisticated prescriptive process. (Following this presentation you will hear more about the Lathrop program from Bruce Bart.)

By the middle of 1972 we felt our diagnostic process was adequate to begin utilizing the results as a needs assessment for program evaluation and modification, and to aid further planning, we tried some scattered results. First, Lathrop Park Youth Camp submitted its diagnostic findings and proved that all of the students within this institution had learning dysfunction. We sampled thirty students at Lookout Mountain School for Boys; all but one had learning problems in various degrees. The astounding part of this sampling was that, according to previous records, 50 percent (or fifteen) of these students had been classified as mentally retarded. Our findings said that only two of them were. We decided to take a comprehensive nine-month sampling beginning at the reception diagnostic center and following students through treatment for validation of findings, and we accordingly prepared a research format and learning disabilities classification procedure. The results of that study bring me here today.

It covers 444 students, all adjudicated committed delinquents or Children in Need of Supervision, who passed through our central diagnostic receiving center from July 1, 1972, to May 1, 1973. Most of them had, prior to the first general release of these statistics, completed at least seven months in follow-up treatment, resulting in such a large degree of validation of the initial findings, that we feel very confident in presenting these results.

First let us identify the basic characteristics of those students (see Figure 2). Their average age is 15.36 years with an average public school grade placement of 8.5, which was approximately one year below chronological age. However, their average grade *functioning* level was 5.8, almost three years lower than the grade placement. The mean public school placement in math and reading was 8.8 while significantly the mean functioning level was 4.6, more than four years lower.

The committed delinquent percentage was 67; 32 percent were CHINS; and 1 percent were federally contracted cases. 75 percent were male; 25 percent female. Some trite generalizations about juvenile institutions were disproved. We found, for example, that only slightly more than one third came from the ghetto and large city areas. Suburban students represented almost another third, and students from rural areas represented slightly less than one third. At the time I was compiling these statistics, I had a research report on my desk which reported that in youth institutions in the western states, 74 percent of the youth came from large city and ghetto areas. What this report failed to show was, as our research indicated, that a large percentage were committed by big city courts, but the student actually came from a rural area. Eighty-four percent of the total number of students were committed by 9 out of 22 judicial districts. Ethnically, more than 50 percent were Anglo, 13 percent were black, 28 percent were Chicanos, 7 percent comprised all remaining classifications.

The most surprising statistic was the family income factor. At the time of this study the average income for the State of Colorado was $8,500 per year per family. Two hundred and one (or 50 percent) of the students in this study came from families which exceeded that average, and of the remaining 223, we could find only 46 that had been identified as welfare cases at the time they were committed. Therefore, we felt we could identify what we might call the typical student in Colorado State institutions.

Figure 2

Statistical Analysis of 444 Students
Average Age 15.36

DELINQUENTS 67%	FEMALES 25%
CHINS 32%	OTHER 1%
MALES 75%	

AREA RAISED		ETHNIC ORIGIN		FAMILY INCOME
122	Rural	Anglo	52%	223 – Below $8,500
149	Suburban	Black	13%	205 – $8,500 to $15,000
165	Urban	Chicano	28%	16 – Over $15,000
8	Other	Other	7%	

A D C 38 OTHER WELFARE 8

One of the first questions we encountered in establishing a format for statistical accumulation of learning disabilities was the myriad variety of possible classifications. Every book seemed to use different words with different definitions. Every specialist seemed to use a different classification. In trying to simplify the procedure to an understandable form, we simply said there were five areas of dysfunction: auditory, visual, language processing, sociological and psychological. Visual and auditory areas could be pretty well defined and identified, but the problems of language processing were, to us, much broader and more numerous than most texts, specialists, and research articles listed and described. Consider the bilingual child, for example. If he has to work in English but uses Spanish as the decoding tool, he certainly has a learning disability problem and would be reflected in these statistics. If, on the other hand, he could decode equally well in both English and Spanish, he has no problem, and would not appear as a language processing statistic. The child that has never mastered the very basic mathematic skills would certainly have a language processing problem in any math program above his basic level. We had a student, for example, who had never mastered the utilization of the number 9. At sixteen years of age, he had learned simply to block out anything dealing with the number 9. When given addition, subtraction, multiplication, even fractions and decimals without a 9 in the problem or a 9 in the answer, he could do it, but he completely ignored any problem containing the number 9. Once this was identified, two weeks of intensive effort cleared up this processing problem. However, he would appear on the statistics as a language processing problem.

I have had a lot of disagreement with public school personnel in regard to the problem of stuttering. We do not consider stuttering a learning disability. Certainly it is an indication of one, but by itself does not present a block to learning and, therefore, is not to be included within the language processing area although the basic cause might appear in other areas.

Social and psychological problems indicated are only those problems which would prevent the child from learning in a meaningful way in the classroom—i.e., the child who cannot function in a group, or one who cannot relate to an adult for learning, or a black who cannot learn from a white, or vice versa. The student who is conditioned to failure and/or the student with an extremely low self image are reflected here. Most of them have either social or psychological problems, but if such problems would not prevent success in learning, these problems would not appear within these statistics. One highly significant fact: 90 percent of those reflected in sociological and psychological problems are also reflected in one or more of the visual, auditory and language processing areas. Which is the causitive factor? We wish we could be sure because other research has indicated that the social or psychological problem resulting from a learning dysfunction cannot be corrected until the learning dysfunction has been corrected.

Basically, then, what I have said concerning classification of learning disabilities is a reflection of our philosophy that a learning disability or dysfunction is anything which prevents a child from achieving successfully in a normal educational setting.

Figure 3 reflects our statistics on learning disabilities and is amplified as follows:

A "mild" classification indicates that the problems could be worked out normally by a regular teacher in a regular classroom provided that the teacher is aware of the problem or dysfunction and could attack it in the correct learning mode and with the correct expectations. Without this, the child will continue falling behind and failing.

"Moderate" problems must have more specialized treatment along with prescriptive individual classroom attention and could not succeed until this is done.

The "severe" problems (and notice the number) must have comprehensive treatment before even trying classroom work. Most of this treatment must be planned and directed by highly qualified specialists.

Figure 3

Of 444 Students

	MILD	MODERATE	SEVERE	TOTAL
Visual	81	81	41	203
Auditory	60	41	17	118
Language Processing	38	106	31	175
Sociological	32	159	112	303
Psychological	41	117	77	235

The totals reflect the magnitude of the job before us. Two hundred and three students out of the 444 have visual problems which require the whole range of individualization and specialized treatment. The same range of treatment is required for 118 with auditory problems, and 175 in the area of language processing. Sociological problems accounted for 303 out of 444 students, and psychological problems numbered 235. Certainly many students are counted twice on the chart—some twice in the same line. However, each one on each line represents a particular problem requiring treatment which must be met before we can term our treatment process a success and before we can realistically expect that student to return to the community to cope with his situation.

In terms of program development, therefore, the total is extremely significant: *90.4 percent* of 444 students within our institutions evidenced a need for special, individualized attention, and all represented problems which could have been caught and treated by community agencies long before they were pushed across our threshold!

A continuation of statistical accumulation through the first of March of 1974, involving 1,296 students, shows that the percentage is constant with few minor changes in the content.

As astounding as this information was to us, we found, as we continued digging into the lives of these 444 students, a number of other significant data. It has been a time consuming task since we have been doing it by hand and are just now getting on a computer, but we have completed the study of a variety of public school records that provides some interesting information.

I found it highly significant that 5 percent had almost identical comments on the elementary school records beginning at the second grade (see Figures 4A through 4E). Look at the first item: truancy. Compare with the pattern of 8 percent of those who started with truancy at third grade and follow in turn with the fourth grade. Two patterns here, but both started with truancy. Fifth grade! Note the jump in percentage to 25 percent and note, also, the first comments on public school records—truancy! Sixth grade followed the same pattern as fifth but the percentage dropped. In a generalization of all of these patterns, two through six, there are at least two significant items common to all—a sudden drop in achiev-

Figure 4A

Behavior Patterns Exhibited by Delinquents with Learning Disabilities

2ND GRADE	
5%	Truancy
	Excessive day dreaming.
	Very much a loner – not interested in physical activities.
	Consistent liar (even when not in defense of self).
	Refused to function in front of other students.
	Verbal abuse to other children (5th grade). Particularly smaller children.
	Failure and refusal to turn in assignments.
	Withdrawal and truancy (6th grade).
	Running away.
	Absolute refusal to try doing school work.
	Truancy and dropout.

Figure 4B

Behavior Patterns Exhibited by Delinquents with Learning Disabilities

3RD GRADE	
8%	Truancy
	Consistent lying.
	Failure to perform in class.
	Verbal abuse to other children (4th grade). Particularly smaller children.
	Continued truancy coupled with runaways.
	Withdrawal from close association with peers.
	Verbal abuse to adults (5th grade).
	Withdrawal – dropout, truancy, runaway (6th grade).

ment coupled with truancy. Twenty-five percent followed no discernable pattern at the elementary level but we have not had time to carry this study through junior high.

I would like to comment very strongly that what we are trying to define in this part of the study is not a classification of potential delinquency but much more important—a red flag and an indicator for schools and communities for early identification of troubled youth. Using such an indicator, intervention could begin early and thus prevent these youngsters from showing up on our institutional statistics.

Another extremely important point, and please do not cite this study without making this clear, the behaviors listed are consistent behaviors and not just occasional ones. Simply because a child is truant does not make him a potential delinquent or a troubled youth.

Figure 4C

Behavior Patterns Exhibited by Delinquents with Learning Disabilities

4TH GRADE	
10%	Truancy
	Highly destructive – particularly classroom items.
	Failure to perform in class – reduced achievement.
	Malicious attacks on younger or smaller children.
	Frequent threats of violence.
	Refusal to perform or answer any questions.
	Concerning his behavior (5th grade).
10%	Truancy and excessive absence.
	Withdrawal from association with peers.
	Malicious actions toward property and others.
	Verbal abuse and threats of violence.
	Rapidly declining grades.
	Refusal to accept teachers as authority figures. (Some obscene phone calls.)
	Failure and withdrawal (5th grade).

Figure 4D

Behavior Patterns Exhibited by Delinquents with Learning Disabilities

5TH GRADE	
25%	Truancy.
	Start falling significantly in achievement.
	Always wanting to sleep.
	Becomes either loner or with small group of failing students.
	Constant behavior aimed at calling attention to self.
	Violence – physical violence or complete detachment – obscene phone calls.
	Long periods of truance and runaway (6th grade).
	Verbal abuse to certain teachers (particularly teachers demanding same level of performance from all students or teachers who stick strictly to text books).

Figure 4E

Behavior Patterns Exhibited by Delinquents with Learning Disabilities

	6TH GRADE
17%	Same behavior.
	General characteristics:
	Sudden dramatic change from good to bad.
	Fast temper – sleep characteristics – verbal or physical abuse.
	Threats of physical violence.
	Runaway and/or truancy – frequent extended absences.
25%	No typical pattern.

What does all this prove? To you, it may prove little. To us it proves many things.

It proves, for example, that the average delinquent simply avoids coping with reality. Beginning failure leads to continuing failure which leads to boredom and/or frustration which, in turn, leads to truancy, drop-out, and possible delinquency. It proves that if you never experienced success, you are sure you can't win and won't try. It proves that youth institutions and youth courts and youth probation and public schools and other community agencies must accept their responsibility to treat these problems evidenced by troubled youth to prevent those youth from living their lives dependent on society's institutions. It proves that we are wrong in institutionalizing youth with problems which the communities should and could handle. It proves that institutional programs should be developed to deliver special services needed by troubled youth which communities cannot provide, and, finally, it proves that there can be no substitute for early intervention.

There you have it! In effect, a five year study development, and let me say that little did we realize five years ago that our effort might have significance beyond our Colorado institutions. Let me say further that none of it could have happened without three primary influences:

1. Title I ESEA.
2. Law Enforcement Agencies Administration.
3. A growing awareness on the part of different segments of the Colorado citizenry on the importance of this kind of effort.

One of these segments, of course, is that whole group of people involved with youth from probation through the judicial courts and institutional personnel. They have all been very important to this development and particularly to the treatment programs that are being developed as a follow-up to this study.

Prior to my coming to the Division, in 1969, 1970, and as recently as 1971, our programs were primarily custodial in nature. Three things have happened to change this:

1. Change in top administration with Jerry Agee moving into the position of Chief of the Division of Youth Services.
2. Information resulting from our efforts in identifying student problems.
3. A growing awareness among our personnel of the needs of students.

These three things have resulted in a reversal of the custodial philosophy, and treatment has now become the criteria. Individualized, fully prescriptive, educational treatment is becoming a reality throughout the Division.

I would like to give you three examples that reflect these changes in the Division of Youth Services in the State of Colorado. Three mini programs have been developed within the last two years (see Figure 5):

Figure 5

Prior to Learning Disabilities Study (EXCEPT FOR LATHROP PARK YOUTH CAMP, ADMINISTRATIVE OBJECTIVES OF THE DIVISION WERE TRADITIONAL)
1. Custody.
2. Protect society.
3. You can't treat them if you don't have them.
4. If you let them escape it's your job.
5. No nosy newspaper reporters permitted.
Since Learning Disabilities Study
1. Keep only those students with problems the community can't handle.
2. Coordinated diagnosis and treatment of learning disabilities as a major thrust.
3. Management by objective.
4. Change yesterday!!!!

1. The Closed Adolescent Treatment Center is a cottage effort to treat highly assaultive, dangerous, and/or markedly suicidal children who have failed in all previous treatments, including a minimum of five institutional programs, and who were certain candidates for either adult correctional institutions or death on the streets. Twenty-four boys and girls in this closed cottage setting receive intensive treatment efforts which appear to be succeeding. This program has not been in existence long enough to have adequate follow-up evaluation, but I say to you it will succeed because the staff will make sure it does succeed!

2. Another program consists of a group of boys and girls with the kind of population with which I am sure you are all familiar. These students are aged 13 through 18 and come on like a second or third grader but are genuinely retarded. Such a youngster is very hungry for attention and affection and is really looking for mothering and apron strings to hang onto. Possibly he is so hungry for these things that he will seek negative attention if no other is available. He has very little feeling of identity or who he is and will, chameleon like, follow almost anyone almost anywhere. Such youngsters are not successful delinquents. In seeking peer approval, they will break all the rules and make adults mad at them, and in seeking adult approval, they will rat on the kids and make their peers furious. They have no internalized standards of what is right and wrong and very little ego strength. They are the students who cause teachers to climb the walls in public school classes. They are the students who cause probation officers and juvenile judges to pull their hair in despair. They need so much so badly and become so dependent that they tend to exhaust the emotional resources of all who come in contact with them. To learn, these youths need a tremendous amount of individual attention, praise, emotional support and warm parenting plus structure. They require very clear and consistent messages about limits and expectations and an overall message that they can succeed and are worthwhile. Put 24 of this kind of population together and add the ingredient of multiple learning disabilities, and you have a group that seems impossible. If we can, in the Total Living Center, develop programs that can be a guide to public schools, to probation and other court entities for working with and remediating this kind of student, we will have done a great service for thousands of people. Most important, we will have intervened in their almost certain deterioration into adult convicts or inmates in mental hospitals.
3. The third program is an intensive treatment center which was formerly a mini-jail for boys who could not exist even in a highly structured closed setting. Lookout Mountain School for Boys is now a highly specialized treatment program which is moving boys back into the mainstream.

The pride of the Division of Youth Services in Colorado is a model program for individualized, prescriptive treatment of troubled youth and a prime example of treatment by prescription. Lathrop Park Youth Camp is located 160 miles south of Denver near Walsenburg, Colorado. Bruce Burt has worked at Lathrop Park Youth Camp since it was constructed in 1967 and, as its principal of education, has been instrumental in developing the educational program which, from what I have seen around the nation, has no equal. It is a fully operational program, ready at any time for observation. All staff members are totally involved and, as a result, follow-up studies of students who have left this program prove it almost 100 percent successful. Mr. Burt was recently moved up to a regional office where he is in a position more effectively to work and plan with schools and agencies in the Southern Colorado area in their commitment to youth. I am sure his message will have great relevance and great interest to this audience.

by
Richard C. Compton

Prescriptive Programming for the Juvenile Delinquent

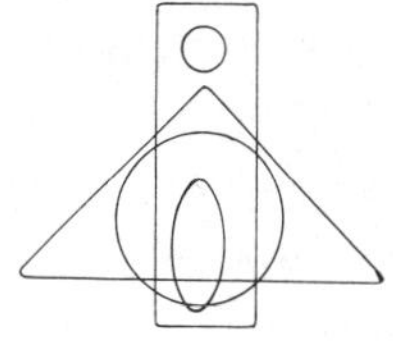

I would like to share with you the story of two young men whom we had in our program. The first young man was of slight build, about 5'2", about 120 pounds, in the ninth grade in a city of about 10,000 in Southern Colorado. He had been placed in a regular ninth grade curriculum. He had a reading ability of second grade, third month, and was a profound discipline problem to the point where the public schools said, "Look, you go home, and we'll call you." This young man had been home 51 days. Finally, a probation officer in another community filed a truancy petition on him because he hadn't been attending school. He went through the standard diagnostic tests, he couldn't read, he would try to read two or three minutes, his eyes would begin to water and turn red, and sometimes he would actually fall asleep. We put him on a reading eye camera. After he had read for three or four minutes, he developed a tremor which kept getting worse and worse and worse until finally he put himself into a state of hypnosis. We took him to the state hospital, had glasses prescribed for him, put him back on the reading eye camera, and lo and behold, no more tremors! We put him into a remedial reading program and brought this youngster up to the expected reading grade in six months. The head of the special education department of the state college, another teacher, and I made the journey to this youngster's community to have a meeting with the principal and with the teachers involved. When we got there, the principal was out getting a haircut and was exceptionally difficult to track down. But we finally got together, explained what we had done, what the problem was, and made some suggestions on how to work with this young man. The principal and the guidance counselor said, "Well, that's all well and good. This is the program we have here. If he fits in, he can stay, and if he doesn't, he leaves." He lasted one month.

The second young man came to us from our children's center. He did not have a mother or father, had been abandoned when he was about three years of age, 6'2" tall, sixteen years old, 190 pounds. At the time we had a small, eight-man football team which competed with some of the smaller schools in the southern part of the state. We put him in a football uniform. He could run the 100 yard dash in 9.6 seconds. We had him two months when we got a call. A gentleman arrived from a Colorado community of 10,000 and said, "You know, we would really like this kid to come to school with us." So we discussed it and sent one of our agents to look at the community and the educational program. They took this young man (and, by the way, there were no other blacks in this community), they found him an apartment, bought him his clothes, gave him meal tickets, provided supervision. This kid, in his first year there, was a leading ground gainer in Triple A football for their school. Their school went on to become Class Triple A champions. He graduated with honors from their high school, and it is my contention that if all our young men were football players, I wouldn't have a job. I'm serious!

It is a sad, sad commentary on the state of affairs as far as American education is concerned. I cannot for the life of me understand why a young man has to be sent to an institution, has to be committed as a delinquent to receive the services which he deserves, which he needs. You know, these kids do learn. We can keep them six months, we put them into the program, and in six months we will have shown an average reading growth of two years. They get a feeling of success; they want to go back to school; they like school. They are away from the daily day in and day out frustrations, the failure. We counsel kids right out of public schools. The public schools do not want them; they don't have programs for them; they cannot meet their needs–or they don't want to meet their needs unless they can run the 100 yard dash in 9.6.

Now I'd like to give a very brief description of the diagnostic prescriptive education model which took about three years to develop. If we were to go through this audience and ask, "What is your idea of juvenile correction," we would probably get two hundred different answers. The next, and most important question, would be, "How do you assess the effectiveness of your program?" Through a Title I grant we called in a group of management people, and we said to them, "Look, there must be something in the area of technology that could help us come up with a program that could meet the needs of these kids." They came up with an answer, and as a result, this is what we did. We established a total treatment program utilizing treatment by objective. Some of you in the business field are aware of management by objective and know that this is nothing new. NASA used this approach to assemble all the efforts of their contractors and subcontractors to bring thousands of parts and hundreds of men together for one goal, one objective, and they were tremendously successful at it. We took the same methodology and applied this to a treatment program.

It would be nice to say that we could be everything to everybody but obviously there are limitations of resources and space. So we hypothesized, "What are the things we know we *can* do?" We came up with 144 objectives which we were sure we could meet. The objectives are composed of separate parts, the first being the goal. Ideally, what would you like to do? Secondly, how are you going to do it, what activities are you going to utilize to meet this goal? Thirdly, what is your specific objective? Fourth, how are you going to know when you have reached this measurement or when you have reached this objective? Lastly, who is accountable? The usual approach is to run through different programs, different assessments, but nobody follows anything up and because everybody is accountable, nobody is accountable. I think this is what is happening in our educational process–no one is accountable. In our particular program, we have established accountability. When a youngster comes into the program, we first determine what he cannot do, and then we determine what he can do and apply these to the 144 objectives. By the time we get these youngsters, it is too late to get back into the remediation aspects. What we want to do is develop adaptive skills. If a youngster cannot learn visually, we will teach him auditorially or tactilely, utilizing the objectives to know where we're at, to let the youngster know where he's at, where we're going, and what our ultimate goal is. This is one of the very essential aspects of the program. The child, himself, must be an integral part of the treatment process. It's easy for us to sit back and say, "We know what's wrong with you, and if you follow our diagnosis, this will be the end result." This means nothing to him. He needs to understand and to make some commitment. Such a commitment comes about merely by making him aware, by saying, "Look, you have an auditory discrimination problem, and consequently you better stay out of classes which lecture—we are going to teach you visually." There's no big mythical process involved here. These kids respond when you approach them with (1) you can learn and (2) you make the commitment, and we'll help you.

In closing, I would like to say that I have heard many, many people make the statement, "If we just had the means, if we just had a way . . ." Well, I say give these kids an opportunity, take them out of the subject-centered, lock-stepped approach that's tied to the Carnegie Unit in the public schools, make them aware of what their problem is, let them work at their own speed, and these kids can learn. Of course, I'm a pessimist when it comes to working with the public schools. I, personally, don't feel that the public schools are ready to change and so what we are doing in Colorado and what we plan to continue to do is to establish alternative education programs in the community. It's easy—no problem—it can be done. We are going to establish alternative education programs in the communities, and we are going to show the local public schools that we can take their failures and teach them in their own communities because they are *their* kids. They aren't ours.

by
Bruce Burt

Developing Vocational Readiness

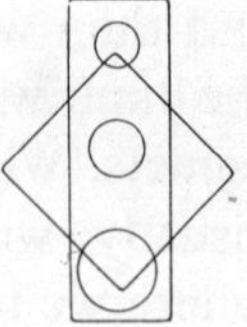

I want to begin by announcing that I've noticed a lot of behavior that I'm not going to be able to accept. I've spoken to the symposium program director and have asked to have monitors spread around the room. The people who have been eating candy and fig newtons–don't come back tomorrow unless you have enough for everybody! You people over there with jackets off–if you can't conform to the community demands of this setting, don't come back tomorrow. There's a fellow back there who is slumping in his seat–if you don't want to pay attention around here, don't come back tomorrow–we'll let somebody else have your seat. You women in slacks, no good, don't come back tomorrow. Have I made my point? By setting arbitrary rules of this sort, I can make everyone in this audience truant and/or delinquent!

My boss, Dr. Ringleheim, Deputy Assistant Director of Education in New Jersey, often used this technique with teachers at Columbia University Teachers College. He would say to his classes, "The first rule is that you have to be inside when the bell rings. The second rule is that the first rule is inoperative–you have to be inside sitting down when the bell rings. The third rule is that you have to be inside sitting down, your mouth shut, and your hands folded on the desk when the bell rings." You can see that at each level there will be more and more people not conforming to the rules. This is called critical demands or community demands. The demands of any given setting will determine how many people are retarded, how many people are delinquent, etc. Can you see how that can happen? I had a complaint from a parent. When I investigated it, I found a teen-aged boy with an IQ in the high 140's who had gotten into some small difficulties in his elementary school. Some well meaning person had seen to it that his record followed him to high school. The precipitating event which made him go bananas was the day in which he had a full period test and was given a zero because he didn't have his textbook. Do you know what would have happened to him if he had opened the textbook during that test? He would have gotten a zero! No wonder kids think they can't win.

I'd like to make several points by telling you some stories. I have two children born after placenta previa, and current HEW research indicates that the correlation between placenta previa, Caesarean section, and all the accompanying complications is .87 with brain damage. So I have two of these kids. A couple of weeks ago the younger of the two had to stay with a friend while my wife was in Washington. The lady took my daughter to the store, and to everyone they met on the way to the store and on the way home from the store, my uninhibited four and a half year old girl announced, "My mommy is sleeping with Mr. Washington." Okay, when is uninhibited behavior no longer cute? When can it be accepted? As a rehabilitation counselor, I once dealt with a very fine woman in the community who had suffered a stroke. In my initial interview, I got nothing but a stream of profanity. A different kind of brain damage, to be sure, but that was about all she could muster. Was her language willful? I'm sure many of you have heard dirty words in the classroom. Are you threatened? Do you throw kids out?

On a Saturday morning several weeks ago, I had to make an hour and a half drive to visit a friend of mine to have my taxes done. I had orders from my wife—I had to "take one of those kids" with me for the day. The oldest one declined, so I asked my son, "Would you like to go?" He said, "Sure!" Now this is the kid who starts to get dressed, I go down and put the kettle on, shave and dress, come back, and he's still staring at his sock. On this fine Saturday, in less than ten minutes Andrew was dressed, an egg shoveled into him and waiting by the car door for me to come out with my box of tax records. What did it cost that boy in terms of effort to be ready in ten minutes? Can he always put forth that much effort? Some day someone is going to do a study, and they are going to come up with a Greek or Latin term for motivation—macro-ergs or some such thing. I choose to call it "Zorks" and just remember that you heard it here first. But the whole subject of motivation is an enormous factor with these kids and certainly needs to be explored. We need to be able to ascertain if a lack of desired behavior is willful or a result of the high cost of concentration or Zorks, if you will.

Then there is the classroom in a town in North Jersey where there had been a Title III grant for operant conditioning. It was a class of neurologically-impaired youngsters (and that's our hardening of the categories title for these kids) whose teacher was absent for the whole month of November with the flu. At the time I visited the classroom, they were using three substitute teachers simultaneously to handle eight kids. I visited it again in May, six months later, and practically every child in that class had been integrated into various aspects of the school program for some part of each day. Necessity is the mother of invention, and it can be done. How much easier it would have been for the school administrator to expel these kids. It's to their everlasting credit that they chose the more difficult route to salvage them.

In New Jersey we are pretty lucky because we do have within the vocational framework a sequence which starts with Technology for Children, something that is peculiar to New Jersey. "Introduction to Vocation" is much the same thing as Dr. Gordon was advocating this morning where people come in from the community to expose the children to different vocational choices.

I have been interested in adaptive behavior in terms of vocation. Studies show that approximately 85 percent of the retarded who lose their jobs do so because of breakdown in adaptive behavior. Some years ago, the American Association for Mental Deficiency and Health, Education and Welfare got together on a project on the "Measurement of Adaptive Behavior." What had happened was in 1959, AAMD came up with a definition and said that a person cannot be identified as retarded by IQ alone. There had to be a measurement of IQ plus a measurement of adaptive behavior. There was only one problem—there was nothing to measure adaptive behavior by. So Dr. Henry Leland and his colleagues set to work at Parsons State Training School in Kansas and began to find some interesting things. They eventually did develop an adaptive behavior scale which has been of great value ever since. In their research, they developed a film of retarded youths behaving. They showed it to different kinds of people who were asked to rate the behavior. Incidentally, the least accepting of the behavior were members of the lower socioeconomic group. You should keep this fact in mind when dealing with possible learning disabled kids from this group. The parents are likely to be unaccepting of childhood behaviors which are beyond the control of the child.

I am kind of the New Jersey State Department of Education's hired gun because it is my job to see that local school districts obey the education laws and also to assist districts in program development. I visited one district to look at classes for 50 percent state reimbursement and toured the schools. The junior high school was an absolute zoo! The walls had been spray painted with unmentionable words and phrases, and it was a disaster area. Then I visited the five-year-old high school which looked as nice and neat as the day it opened. In the junior high school there was a class of fourteen quote educable retarded unquote boys who were supposed to move into the high school in the fall. We all agreed that the critical demands, the community demands, of that high school were such that the junior high kids would last about forty minutes of the first day of school and be gone forever. We decided that we had to do something in order to prepare those students for the fact that there was a dress code in the high school as well as some other aspects which would indicate "undesirable visability," as Henry Leland would say, which is, after all, what adaptive behavior is all about.

We applied for and received a Title VI grant of $4,500. In the project group, 26 percent of the students had been arrested; there was a low of one and a high of nine run-ins with the police. They averaged 20 percent absenteeism during the school year, were chronically late, chronically inept. A couple of them couldn't—or didn't—dress themselves, couldn't get their own breakfasts, and this was the gang that was scheduled to go into high school. Using the Title VI grant, a summer program was constructed to begin changing their behavior and provide them with the social cues that Dr. Brutten mentioned earlier.

How many of you have heard a secondary teacher say, "I don't want any of those kids in my class." Sound familiar? The director of the summer program was very shrewd—he got hold of the high school shop teacher, an old hand, to teach the summer program. The kids had swimming and gym, and immediately there were some cultural and psychological problems because the kids didn't want to get undressed and take a shower. It was solved by having staff members shower with them and by some very frank discussions and explanations about individual differences. They also got academics, and you must understand that except for one curve breaker who was reading at the sixth grade level, most of these kids were reading on the second or third grade level. They considered what they were being given "baby stuff."

The parents got some counseling, and the students got counseling from a school social worker who also went out to their homes and held reveille for those who were not there by the specified starting time in the morning. The social worker literally went into the homes, into the bedrooms, and said, "Get up!" Saw to it that they got up, dressed, and reported to school. In the afternoon, every one of the kids had a job which was arranged through the Community Action Program in that particular municipality. Now, 1974, three years later, one child has moved to Puerto Rico and has left the program, but there have been zero dropouts. The kids have been taking part in the reading lab program available in the school with fair progress in reading. There has been little or no truancy or tardiness. Until this spring there were no further run-ins with the law until one member of the class had a brush with the police, and we think it will get ironed out. I was there recently for my official visit, again scrutinizing programs for approval of the 50 percent state money. I visited that room, and there were marvelous things going on, kids interested and vital. They showed me a video tape of interviews they had conducted with personnel people in the community, and they were sitting there picking the interviews apart and seeing how they could have done better. It has obviously been a good program, no dropouts, no more truancy, no more brushes with the law. Why? What happened? Personally, I feel that the program met the individual needs of those kids. There was an immediate pay-off for appropriate behavior throughout the program by social acceptance from the staff. There was an immediate pay-off by having money in the pocket from the afternoon jobs. There was no artificial hassel, no community demands that they had to meet over the summer. Yes, the social worker went out and jostled them out of bed and got them into school because he cared, but nobody got expelled from the program because he said a dirty word or was late or whatever. The goal was *to keep them in school, not to find reasons for expelling them from school.* I think that's the big difference.

In New Jersey we have quite a good special education law. The heart of it is that each school board shall identify, classify, and place all handicapped children between the ages of five and twenty. Unfortunately, many teachers think that is just grand because they can refer troublemakers to the Child Study Team, get them out of their classes and not have to worry about them any more. In terms of the kinds of problems we are discussing today, and as much as it is my job to see that the New Jersey law is followed to the letter, I just wonder how much of a favor we are doing some of those children because, as Henry Leland has observed, "How can you learn to adapt to a community if you have been removed from the community or never allowed to enter it?"

by
Charles A. Weening

What Do You Think?

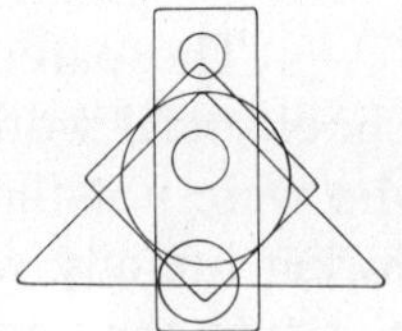

Aloha! I've come a long way to participate in this conference, and it is a distinct pleasure to be here. I come from Hawaii, rather a small state, with a total population of 800,000, and my jurisdiction in comparison to mainland standards is not very large. The First Circuit Court in the State of Hawaii encompasses the Island of Oahu, which is the island upon which Honolulu is located, with a jurisdictional population of about 600,000. Our problems are the problems of small "big" cities, the same problems that you have here on the mainland. We, too, have good psychologists and poor psychologists, good probation officers and poor probation officers, good lawyers and poor lawyers, judges who are adequate, judges who are inadequate, and judges who are superior.

I have always viewed the law as a tool. That may differ from other people who view the law as something that was written on two tablets of stone on Mt. Sinai. That's not my attitude of the law. Law is made by people who are elected by you. If you don't like the people who make the law, then if you change the people, you may change the law. I view the practice of law as a manipulation of the system of law because lawyers work within a legal system which your decision makers in the legislature have created. By registering to vote and casting ballots, you decide who your legislators are and what laws will be passed. You allow, through laws, the kind of abuse of justice that you heard Mr. Mangel describe because the laws in those states he visited allow those kinds of practices. Not the judges. The laws! Through laws, you have allowed or limited the judges' dispositions in deciding cases and you have also, by not giving your human services sufficient funds, prevented youth in trouble from receiving a full spectrum of services. You have allowed the priorities in society to focus upon athletics, for example, as an area in which a vast amount of money will be spent, while very little will go to the delivery of human services to children.

In situations where government is experiencing a tightening of the belt, where do the cuts occur? The cuts occur in children's programs. They do not occur even in the programs which deal with penology applicable to adults. They occur first in the area of juvenile justice. Why? Well, let me ask a question. Do the kids vote? Let me ask another question. Are they banded together in a pressure group which allows them at least to go to the legislature and present testimony? The answers are obvious–a resounding no! They don't vote, they don't have a pressure group–but for the gentlemen on this symposium and others like them, the kids don't have a voice that clamors and begs for help.

This whole business of labeling–special education, compensatory education, juvenile delinquent, CHINS, MINS, JINS, whatever–is done by adults. These are the labels our speakers here have used in order to best and most conveniently describe a situation, and I use them, too. But, you know, kids don't understand CHINS, MINS, and all the rest of the adult nomenclature. I'm really happy that I am in a family court because I don't have to call a kid CHINS, MINS, or delinquent. In my adjudication, I can simply say the child comes within the jurisdiction of the court–period! When I do that, it opens up another avenue to me in what we call a bifurcated hearing. That second part being–what do I do with a child. Again, the laws that your legislators make, and my legislators make, either limit me or any other judge, or they allow us to exercise as much discretion as possible. Discretion can be a very terrible word, or it can be a very good word.

In the State of Hawaii, we are not limited to probational commitment. The Family Court Act is broad enough so that I am limited only by my imagination and my ingenuity. Of course, any decisions or dispositions are not made in my own head without support of evidence on the record because, you see, I am really a lawyer in disguise when I wear my robe. I know that if I make a mistake or if someone is dissatisfied with my decision, he can always go to the Supreme Court, which is the only body that can limit my decision. If I have made an error (and I don't commit error on purpose–nobody does) then the Supreme Court will have to tell me that I have committed error. But the record must be clear in case there is dissatisfaction.

And so I use, in the State of Hawaii and in my court, whatever services are available to identify the person who is before me–not a child but a person. The whole philosophy of the juvenile justice system as opposed to the adult justice system is individualized justice, to tailor a disposition to the child. I am not only talking about children with learning disabilities. This concept of individualized justice is so important that those in adult penology and in the adult justice system are seeking to inculcate that kind of attitude and philosophy in the adult courts.

Certainly, if one can adopt the philosophy of individualized justice, then a judge who is, in fact, very conscientious about what is going on, will attempt to learn what services are available within the community and what kind of measuring devices are available so that the best possible assessment can be made of the person before him. I frequently use chromosome screens to find out if a child has a chromosome defect. This approach came into prominence when Richard Speck, the mass murderer, was discovered to have had a chromosome defect. As a result, someone got a grant and made extensive chromosome examinations in all the prison systems and learned that a great percentage of those incarcerated had chromosome defects. Of course, that doesn't mean that everybody who has a chromosome defect is in prison.

Psychoneurological tests are also very, very important to me because they indicate that this person before me is very special and must be dealt with in a very special way. And so I use psychiatrists, psychologists, counselors. I also use workers at my detention facilities who are not college trained to provide me with input on an individual child with whom I have not yet been able to establish rapport. People who are not professionals can give it straight, too, can give their observations to me in language I can understand instead of the special language used by professionals.

The problem with all of these kinds of assessment of the individual appearing before me for disposition arises when I look to the professionals afterwards, and I say, "Where is a program?" Do you know what they say? They say, "Well, we don't know what to do." And I reply, "Well, do not curse the judge for not doing anything if you haven't provided me with something to do something with. Your job is to get me a program. I'm a judge–just a simple country lawyer." So I look to the professionals, pleading for a program, waiting, waiting, and nothing happens. Occasionally, someone does come up with a really meaningful program, one that at least meets my immediate needs and, more importantly, the child's immediate needs. When that happens, by gum, that child goes into that program but first that child or that person is told why and is allowed to interchange. When I tell a child that a psychologist is going to talk to him, to evaluate him, the usual reaction is, "I'm not going to talk to a shrink–I'm not a mental case." So I take the time to sit down with a youngster and say, "Look, I've talked to psychologists, a lot of judges and psychologists talk to psychiatrists, and psychiatrists talk to God, and I don't think I am a mental case, am I?" And the kid looks at me and says, "No." Of course, I don't know if he is really saying what he believes or not. Then I say, "The psychologist is going to talk to you about your strengths and your weaknesses so that we might promote your strengths and perhaps help you with your weaknesses in order to help you get over the situation you're in." None of the children, when I have explained the reason for a psychological evaluation, have objected to talking with a psychologist or a psychiatrist. Kids understand. They really do. You have to trust them. I do!

After the assessment is made, then the disposition must be tailored to the individual child. It may interest you to know that I get the most resistance from the adults who come to court. The people who are supposed to be helping these children object to any novel way for dealing with a specific child. Social workers have come up to me and said, "You can't do that. It's never been done before." Am I bound by history? Consistency is the sin and the vice of the unimaginative. And so we deal with the child in the manner we think best and hope that the social worker will come along.

Obviously I have an attitude that the court, the law, must meet the needs of the times. Obviously I believe in an aggressive kind of court. The value of a court is really tenfold, not only in the decisions the judge makes but also in the philosophy that the court causes to permeate the community. A judge, just by his attitude and philosophy, can stifle novel actions brought before him because, whether you know it or not, the judge controls the court. When he tells a lawyer to sit down, that lawyer sits down. And if the judge allows the community to understand that, in fact, he will entertain novel actions, then those suits which will help youth in trouble, including children with learning disabilities, will come to his court.

Yesterday the right to treatment and the right to education were mentioned. These rights are going to be established. I predict that within the next six to twelve months, the next state to decide that issue specifically will be the State of New York when it moves on the right to treatment in the area of mental health. On Tuesday the Dallas Morning News carried a long article about a class action suit brought by the Dallas Legal Services Offices in order to force the people at the Terrell State Hospital to provide humane treatment for the patients. Now, by God, if those people in the Legal Services Offices can file that kind of suit, surely they can also file a class action suit to get an answer on whether or not children with learning disabilities have a right to education in the State of Texas. Why haven't they done so? Maybe no one has asked them to. You should! If there is one thing that comes out of this symposium, it should be a resolution to contact the Dallas Legal Services Offices and say, "Would you please entertain a class action suit to establish the right to education for children with learning disabilities?"

Some of our kids who have come before the courts have gone to our legislature and given testimony. One kid went to court one day and in responding to the education committee, he said, "You know, gentlemen, school should be better than drugs but it's not. It's a bummer." And he was right. For him, a push-out not a drop-out, school was, indeed, a bummer. It seems to me that school, any educational system, can be a good experience if you and your community can develop the attitude that it is *your* school, not a school that belongs to the school board or the school district. There are some principals who think that it is their school, and some school boards who think that it is their school board. It is *your* school board, and I think that the courts could establish whose school board it is and whose school it is if the situation were directly presented to them. At least you would have the question decided once and for all. If you never ask, you will never know.

I hope my remarks have given you hope and perhaps placed in focus the many thoughts expressed at this symposium. I have enjoyed my participation in this important forum. The State of Texas is, indeed, huge, and the hearts of its people are great. I go back to Hawaii with warm feelings.

by
Patrick K.S.L. Yim

The Learning Disabled Adolescent

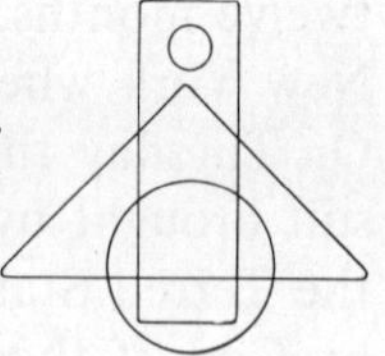

I would like to begin my remarks about "Where do we go from here?" with a brief description of where I have been in terms of my own professional training and experience. I finished a fairly traditional psychoanalytically oriented child psychiatry residency in 1970. During the last year of that residency, however, I became increasingly dissatisfied with purely psychogenic explanations for the many behavior disorders and learning problems that were being presented to our clinic staff. I began to read on my own, and I began to consult with other child psychiatrists who had become knowledgeable in the field of learning disability and minimal brain dysfunction.

When I entered the Public Health Service (in lieu of military service) in 1970, I was initially sent to the NIMH Clinical Research Center at Lexington, Kentucky, for the treatment of narcotic addiction. As I arrived in these surroundings, I found myself totally at a loss to communicate with these people. Some of my best in-service training came from my patients at Lexington who were addicts. I realized that much of my professional jargon and my intellectual understanding of psychodynamics was largely irrelevant. I had to learn entirely new ways of understanding these people, and I learned for the first time what it is like to grow up in a delinquent and deviant sub-culture.

After one year in Lexington I was transferred to the Fort Worth Clinical Research Center. Shortly after I arrived there, this Center was transferred to the Bureau of Prisons and became a minimum security institution, the Federal Correctional Institution at Fort Worth, Texas. While this facility is very radical in terms of its humanitarian reforms, including the presence of both men and women in the prison setting, I nevertheless felt frustrated in my 18 months of working there. The reasons for my frustration centered around the fact that I do not feel that significant and lasting behavioral changes can be made as long as a person is incarcerated even if the walls are painted fuchsia and aquamarine and even if there is a mall, a gazebo, and strolling guitars. The simple fact is that people are locked up and stripped of many of the usual human privileges.

I was amazed time and time again in my work with addicts and younger drug abuse patients to find a history which was consistent with the hyperactive child syndrome and with the development of a learning disability. Many of these young people had begun to use amphetamines, and it is my suspicion that what they were doing was self-medicating themselves with a stimulant medication which is known medically to have salutary effect in children who have minimal brain dysfunction. The abuse potential, however, is highly significant, and by the time these young people had reached adolescence, they had developed a very negative attitude either toward themselves or toward the larger society. As I have followed many of these children, I have detected that during the first six or seven years of school their attitude seems to be (in terms of transactional analysis) "I'm not O.K., you are O.K." There seems to be a switch sometime during adolescence, however, and the new position is "I'm O.K., you're not O.K." This is the position from which many delinquents operate, and I see it as a defensive and reparative maneuver because they have been overwhelmed through years of school failure, frustration, and parental hassling by these not O.K. feelings. As I observed these young people, many of whom had committed major crimes and felonies and were incarcerated, I began to think that much more attention needed to be given to the problem of learning disability prior to and during the crucial adolescent years. I left the Correctional Institution to become the part-time Medical Director of the Drug Treatment Center and the part-time psychiatric director at the Child Study Center. It is from these two bases of operation that I have worked in the community, and I feel that I am in a fairly good position to describe the kinds of activities that are going on locally.

In the first place, I think that far too little is going on locally. It would be much easier for me to list all of the problems and be a wailing Jeremiah. I do not think that this is the most constructive approach. It is true that there is lack of communication between school systems and agencies. It is true that there is lack of a coordinated system for the delivery of health cares to children and adolescents. It is true that there is relative isolation of law enforcement groups. However, there have been changes within the past year, and some of these groups are coming together. I will describe the local involvement to reach the learning disabled child and the child who is a high risk for incarceration and adjudication.

When I began at the Child Study Center I met a staff primarily non-medical and primarily psychoanalytic in orientation. As a result of at least a year of intensive training and supervision, every social worker there knows just about all there is to know about minimal brain dysfunction. There is now an MBD clinic which provides diagnosis, medical supervision, follow-up, and liaison with the school system. I have not yet been able to convince the psychologists that minimal brain dysfunction is a live entity, but you can't win them all.

Another change that we made at the Child Study Center was to revise our method of intake. The so-called "sacred cow of the child guidance intake" was put out to pasture. No longer did a family have to first interview the social worker, then six weeks later see the psychologist, then perhaps six months later see the psychiatrist. We decided to do intakes in groups with social workers interviewing the families and with me as the psychiatrist floating from one family to another, performing necessary tasks as indicated by the initial intake interview. This meant that I would sometimes do several neurological examinations in one morning and would start several children on medication on the same day as they came to the clinic. This proved to be very profitable and expedited our services greatly.

Most of what I have described was designed for work with the younger child. We also began to look around at our adolescent population and we found a tremendous number of adolescent learning disabled children with very low self esteem who were getting into acting out antisocial behavior. We decided to initiate a program of recreational therapy or therapeutic recreation, and the reasons for our doing this were several. In the first place, we realized the difficulty of the learning disabled child in verbalizing and conceptualizing his problems. Many of these children have lower verbal I.Q.'s than performance I.Q.'s and have great difficulty in expressing abstract ideas. We felt that it was relatively useless to place these children in traditional psychotherapy groups. Another reason for our recreation program was the reluctance of almost all adolescents to discuss problems with a professional therapist. This reluctance is combined with an opposition to being seen by a psychiatrist and thus labeled "crazy."

Thus, we devised therapeutic recreation groups staffed by what would normally be called "paraprofessionals." Some of these had bachelor's degrees and some did not. They met with the children once or twice weekly and received concentrated psychiatric supervision during the period of time that the recreation groups were meeting. The results have been to us very encouraging. We have been able to see dramatic improvement in school attendance and even in school performance because of the freeing up of some of the anger and also because of the feeling that here was a group to which they could belong. The Child Study Center has been so satisfied with the program that it is now going into a day camp program for the summer which will culminate in a two-week residential camp. The whole concept of recreational therapy is one which should seriously be considered by anyone who is working with the learning disabled adolescent.

I left the Child Study Center in March to become full time Medical Director of the Tarrant County Medical Education and Research Foundation. This is a rather unique local private, non-profit foundation. I am the only medical person on the staff (you might say the "token doctor") and we are involved in two major areas, (1) the treatment of problems related to substance abuse and (2) the provision of direct mental health services to young people in our county. We also think of what we do as prevention but we do not ordinarily call it that because of grant and funding requirements. Although many people have said that the heroin epidemic is over and although there is some sentiment in the country which is optimistic about problems of substance abuse, I do not necessarily share this optimism. We are currently seeing 17 and 18-year-old heroin addicts. These are not necessarily children from the ghettos or the barrios. They are also from affluent middle class white high schools. We have an out-patient program, and we maintain an outreach center in a black, a brown, and a white neighborhood. We have an in-patient residential therapeutic community for persons 17 and over, and we are now negotiating for funds to operate a treatment center for young persons age 10 to 17. There is at the present time no such treatment facility in Tarrant County. We have had numerous meetings with school officials and other agencies, and we are currently optimistic that we will be able to open the center sometime this summer.

We see it as a short to medium term residential facility where a child can receive a thorough educational, psychiatric, neurological, and psychological evaluation and where there can be a clear assessment of what is going on with the family. We will be happy to provide results to you at the next meeting of this symposium as to how we are progressing.

I've talked about the local scene and I've talked about programs. There are many larger questions to be asked, however, which are unrelated to the small program which we hope to initiate. I think that these larger questions relate to what the learning disabled adolescent and the young person in general feel in relationship to our society. I talk with many of these youngsters both in my practice and outside of it. The main feelings which come across to me, and if there is anything that you take away from the conference I would like for you to consider these two feelings very strongly, are (1) oppression, and (2) powerlessness. The learning disabled adolescent particularly feels the very oppressed environment. He is often scapegoated; there is often prejudice against him; he is often referred to as a "dumb-dumb" or as a "retard"; he is forced to go into tutoring situations whether he wants to or not; he is taken from one evaluation center to another, and is often left feeling totally powerless as to having any alternatives as to what will be done to him. These two feelings of oppression and powerlessness leave these young people with a feeling that there is "no exit." It seems to them as though they can go into the system and become somewhat dehumanized in the process or they can drop out of the system and the usual alternative to dropping out or being pushed out of the system is the counterculture with its heavy emphasis upon drugs. Drugs are marvelous antidepressants and euphoriants. They allow people to cope with years of frustration, rage, envy, guilt, and anxiety. The problem with drugs as a coping mechanism, however, is that they pose even greater problems for the person who uses drugs. There must be other answers to these kinds of problems.

I was privileged to attend a meeting in Chicago in March where I heard Dr. Roberto Belmar, the former Director of National Health Services in Chile. His remark at that meeting which impressed me was "Young people are the critical conscience of the society. They are the only ones who have the capacity to see the world." My translation of this is that young people are the only ones who see the obvious. They are the ones who request their parents to "tell it like it is." You can recall this theme in the story of the emperor's new clothes. As the story goes, everyone in the population is admiring the emperor's new clothes which are, of course, nonexistent. The only person who has the temerity to point out that the emperor is naked is a very small boy who jumps up and says, "The emperor has no clothes on at all!" We are not given the details of what happens at the end of this story. It seems to me there are two options. One option is that everyone turns around, beats him on the head, kicks him out of school, and sends him to the back of the bus, or perhaps to a juvenile detention center. The other option is that some people in the crowd begin to agree with him and say, "You know, you're right; he really doesn't have any clothes on, and I wonder what can be done about it."

It is in this context of seeing the obvious that I mention my favorite quotation from my favorite story. It is from St. Exupery's *The Little Prince.* The quotation is as follows: "And now here is my secret, a very simple secret. It is only with the heart that one is able to see rightly. What is essential is invisible to the eye." I would say, then, that as we work with these adolescents, we need to be able to see with the heart. I would raise these larger questions which seem to me to stand apart from programs, apart from educational and instructional devices, and apart from many of the formal mechanisms of our educational, mental health, and juvenile justice systems. I will leave the questions unanswered and will let each of you answer them in his own way. Here are the questions:

1. How does the young person feel important or needed in our society?
2. Do young people experience any political power whatsoever?
3. Do they have the opportunity to create beauty?
4. Are they taught to negotiate the system?
5. Do they have optimal opportunities for health care?
6. Do they have real training to prepare them to work in the world or is this a sham?
7. Is there opportunity for meaningful communication with adults and with peers?

I do not have the answers to all of these questions. All of you here are obviously interested in the problems of youth in trouble or you would not be at this meeting. I think that we must continually introspect, however, to see whether we are trying to find answers to these questions. Are we stepping stones or stumbling blocks? Are we part of the solution or are we part of the problem? Are our programs, our policies, and our personal lifestyles nourishing and life giving, or have we become toxic and poisonous? In short, do we really give a damn about what happens to children who are "the world's greatest resource, and the only hope for the future of mankind?"

I will close my presentation by making eight practical suggestions which are sort of off the top of my head and which will certainly need refinement should they ever come into resolution form. The eight practical suggestions are as follows:

1. Repeal laws which require compulsory school attendance.
2. Repeal child labor laws so that children can go to work before they are 16.
3. Require courses in learning disabilities for teacher certification.
4. Educate doctors, attorneys, judges, and school administrators in the problems of the learning disabled child.
5. Create alternative school systems outside the traditional system.
6. If you don't mind losing your job, work guerrilla style within the system.

7. Vote for candidates for public office who put the needs of children at a very high priority.
8. Don't give up the ship.

by
Julius Collum

"As I Was Saying . . ."

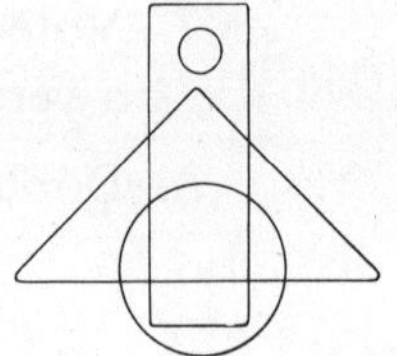

CHESTER POREMBA

This morning each of our speakers is going to have an opportunity to, as we say in show biz, "wing it," to make any comments he wishes, to elaborate on what he said yesterday. We have all been besieged in the halls and corridors yesterday and today, and we want to comment on the various responses and questions which have been asked of us.

We made a case yesterday. We are not here to prove learning disabilities are here to stay. We are not here to prove delinquency is here to stay. The case we made is that most of the delinquents in this country are really learning disabled kids who have never been treated, never been helped. Even if we could reach and identify every child at kindergarten or first grade level, I doubt if we have the manpower in education to save all the kids. So, in my lifetime, I don't see eradication of the problem. But I do hope in my lifetime we can begin to see a philosophy develop which will insist that every child deserves an education which he can handle, one which will be relevant and meaningful to him in his life. I hope that fifteen years from now there will be no need for this kind of symposium and no need for special education because it is my dream–and I am sure yours–that all of education will be very special for every kid.

You have heard the figures, and I think they are accurate, that 85 to 90 percent of delinquent youngsters have learning disabilities. You have also heard that 20 to 25 percent of the school population have learning disabilities. Those, I think, are very significant figures. We do not mean to imply that all learning disabled kids will become juvenile delinquents. They have other ways to act out. I see some of the other ways in Children's Hospital. I am convinced that more than 50 percent of the very young drug addicts, as young as ten or eleven, are learning disabled kids. And then there are also the kids who fade into the woodwork, who disappear from the scene. There are thousands of such kids in this country who emerge eventually on welfare rolls and in various other such places.

We have also been hearing during this symposium that it costs an awful lot of money *not* to do something for these kids. Crime costs you $8,000 for each delinquent in your state each year. As he grows older and more of a criminal, he will cost you $27,000 a year. Each criminal career will cost you one-half million dollars–$250,000 on this side of the court and $250,000 in terms of property loss, etc. And although we talk about dollars and cents, there is no way we can put a price, as our speakers have said, on human dignity and human life.

HAROLD LEVY

We received a nice press in the morning newspaper, and I'm grateful for everything that was written, but I would like to refute two items. The headline said, "Delinquency and Learning Link, Official Says." I looked to see who the official was, and it was me! I'm not an official! I have some titles from volunteer work of which I am very proud, but I want to stress that the work which my colleagues and I are doing is done as private practitioners of medicine. The family doctor, the family pediatrician, really has the key to early recognition. He is the only member of the team who can go into the newborn nursery and see this potential future learning-disabled child. He can follow him as an infant, through his developmental stages. He can see what happens to him at the beginning of school, and he can build rapport and understanding and warmth with the parents which is irreplaceable. I'd like to make my pitch for the importance of the family doctors and to urge parents to involve their family doctors and family pediatricians.

The second point in the newspaper article which I would like to refute is the quote "sedatives are great." Let me clarify that. We are using a certain group of medications which are not tranquilizors and which are not sedatives. I guess the best descriptive term we could use would be "organizers" which seem to help these children pull things together better. They think more clearly, and they seem to be able to attack a task and complete it better, not while they are under the influence of this medication but while this medication stimulates them to be better able to control their impulses and their attention span. Tranquilizers and sedatives are not the answer. We are not trying to zonk these kids out so they quit annoying the teacher or quit bugging the mother. We are trying to let these children utilize what talents they have to better advantage. I don't know a medication in the world which will raise a child's I.Q. one tenth of a point, but I have seen children raise themselves six or seven levels in reading or in math when the proper medication is administered. Fortunately, these medications are relatively safe. They do have some side effects, as even aspirin does, and they should be carefully supervised by physicians. I am convinced that without medication many of these youngsters would be irrevocably lost, and there are many mothers who would say "Amen!" to that! I do believe that we must be judicious, and we must be willing to try other medications to see which ones will be most useful.

Fortunately, the medications we are using are not habit forming. Since Dr. Bradley's first report in 1937, there has not been a single case in the medical literature of any child's ever becoming addicted or any habituation to these medications. It is unfortunate that our knowledge of the chemistry of learning and memory had to surface at the same time as the drug problem because, unfortunately, there are many parents who have been criticized by neighbors and well meaning in-laws. "You took your child to the doctor, and he put her on drugs? That adorable little thing?" Well, that adorable little thing is terribly frustrated because she's not achieving in the classroom. The most rewarding experience I've had in twenty five years of pediatric practice is when a child called me up at home and read me his report card. Or a father called and said, "Not only did Bobby's teacher call tonight and say he is making all B's this six weeks–and after all those D's and F's you know what that means–but the great thing was when she said, 'I wish you could see how proud the other children are of how much better Bobby's doing in school'." That's what we are shooting for–self esteem, self respect. We are not trying to put these children under the influence of something which will make them less aware of reality as, indeed, tranquilizers or sedatives might. We are trying to use something which will make them actually more aware of reality, more aware of their faculties and more capable of performing.

Another important point I'd like to make is that for a long time we have talked about the paradoxical effect of these medications in that the stimulants appeared to act as sedatives or tranquilizers, that when children went through adolescence, they outgrew learning disabilities or minimal brain dysfunction so medication could be stopped, and, finally, that one never sees a hyperactive adult! Well, there certainly are hyperactive adults, thank goodness, because these are the people who are the real leaders. It's when hyperactivity is channeled into a particular goal that it becomes an asset rather than a liability. But it is important that we realize that minimal brain dysfunction does not magically disappear with adolescence and adult life. As we get to be adults, we can hide some of our difficulties. You don't have to know I was such a klutz and played right field, as I mentioned yesterday. I don't have to go to the swimming pool and show what an un-Mark Spitz I am. I can get into fields of endeavor by which I can make these deficits less apparent. As adults, we don't necessarily have to deal with competition but in school every single, grinding day our children are surrounded by twenty five or thirty competitors who are there to criticize, ridicule, and laugh at failure. Even if not ridiculed, the child himself knows if he is not succeeding.

We must examine this whole problem in the light that if we, as doctors, see an adolescent who has had a history of problems in school and we put him through a neurological examination and find nothing, that still does not exclude the possibility that he has minimal brain dysfunction in some subtle form. These things are difficult to detect medically, and they don't hold up to the usual rules of detection. Many of the diagnostic devises we use are not too valuable, and when the adolescent has outgrown his left and right confusion and some of his body part identification mix-ups and his handwriting isn't quite so distorted, go back and find out what he was like in the first grade. As we said yesterday, parents will tell you that most of these youngsters who are being expelled and suspended from school started out with trouble in the very first grade. And this is where we must focus if we are to help the learning disabled adolescent.

MILTON BRUTTEN

I would like to talk a little more about something I mentioned yesterday and then take a stratospheric leap into a line of investigation involving learning disabilities, delinquency, and creativity which I feel would be very worthwhile to pursue on a new frontier.

I have been intrigued over the years in working with learning disabled adolescents to find the sudden paradoxic appearance, unanticipated by anything we did with the youngster in the educative process in a reasonably good special school and unpredicted by anything which appeared on formal psychological tests, of what I called yesterday the "flare" or the "bent" or the "genius" of the child.

I recall, for example, one boy at our school who is not so hot academically, can't interpret a lot of social cues, but put him in a fishing stream, a trout stream, and he is able somehow to read the surface of the water. I stand there and can't see a thing, but he is able to detect subtle little clues from the surface of the water that are not apparent to anybody else. Where this ability, this skill, came from nobody knows. I recall another youngster, a girl, who loves to be with horses and who has an extraordinary facility for gentling a wild horsc and helping that horse to calm down. She is really a marvelous trainer of animals. I have seen other young people where a totally unanticipated artistic flare has suddenly occurred. I tell the story often about a youngster at Vanguard School who used to whittle surreptitiously under his desk. This whittling was a threat to the teachers. It stood in the way of something the English teacher was trying to impart or something that the social studies teacher was trying to convey. (So very often in a structured school situation, an attempt is made on the part of well-meaning teachers to re-direct, reroute, or even suppress the flare or the gift.) In the case of this young person with a flare for whittling, we found some vocational attributes later on which utilized this skill. He is now working in a dental laboratory in the Philadelphia suburbs, carving molds of models of false teeth and having a very productive career.

By now, you have gathered that I have a particular, personal interest which seemingly has very little to do with my professional concerns for learning disabled children. I look at and collect crazy, wild, far-out, contemporary art. What's that got to do with learning disabilities? Maybe a lot! Most of my friends are people who are non-standard thinkers. I gravitate toward artists, and I find that some interesting things characterize these people. I have found in talking with them about their early lives what seems to be an unusual incidence of what we might call, if we had seen these people when they were kids, learning disability. Many of them had trouble spelling, many still do, many can't write or do math, many are slow, inefficient readers. So here are some of the young people who are the outstanding and creative spirits of our day who may have been learning disabled.

I find, also, an unusual occurrence in these people of a polarity which I was discussing with Dr. Berman. Dr. Berman is a man who is interested in carrying on a line of investigation which happens to converge with some observations of my own. I find an unusual polarity of extraordinary rigor and orderliness which is very compulsive, and, at the same time, a peculiar bent or what I call a "wild gleam in the eye." I'll be talking next Sunday afternoon with a young man who is a drop-out from medical school, who has an extraordinarily rigorous scientific background which is still important in his life and in his work. He has had evidence of learning disability. All of a sudden, as I talk to this young man, some wild, far-out speculation will occur to him which takes him off into the blue skies, and I love to follow him there.

Let's speculate and let's say there is a possibility, at least among certain young people who are learning disabled, that a creative flare exists which goes far beyond the usual. These young people who produce artistic works, music, poetry, painting, sculpture, whatever it is that can be exciting, enrich our lives and redirect our way of looking at life into unaccustomed paths. That's what I think the good artist does—he changes our vision. Now, is it possible that, in some cases at least, if a young person gets into the hands of a learning disability specialist who tries to structure him and direct him one way or another, we may well meaningly squelch the creativity of this individual, just as my teacher tried to do with the young man whose whittling interferred with the English class? Is that a possibility? I would like to propose an investigation of this premise, a line of research to investigate and look into the relationship between delinquency, creativity, and learning disability. But for the immediate future one of the best things we can do, in a practical sense, to stave off dissatisfaction, unhappiness, uneasiness, and lack of self regard in our adolescents and to reduce the tendency of some learning disabled young people to turn to antisocial behavior, is to try desperately to be open as teachers, as probation workers, as parents, open to all of the options within the child's natural make up, that "wild gleam in his eye" which makes him head in a direction which parents and teachers may not see as valuable. I talked about this to a group in Pittsburgh a few weeks ago, and one mother, a lovely lady, got up and said, "Well, my child has no interests whatsoever! What are you going to do about a youngster who isn't interested in anything?" I asked her, "What does your boy do with his free time. How does he get his kicks? What does he get pleasure from?" This is something very important to ask every teenager. It turned out that he writes crazy, pseudo-science fiction stories. I asked, "Why isn't that of interest to you?" "Well, he's not doing his homework when he's doing that." I find that parents often have in mind a set of limited options to which they want to direct their youngster because those are the options which they feel will lead to the child's success in life. I have spoken often about the student I had at Vanguard School who loved to practice magic tricks. His parents were distressed about this because he was practicing far into the night when he should have been studying. A constant battle was waged between the child and his parents because he wanted to do something which he found fun but which teachers and parents did not feel to be of value because it could not, in their minds, lead to college, to something which would be vocationally useful or socially acceptable.

And so I say please, please look at each youngster with total freshness and openness. Expose him to a variety of experiences and situations. If you don't have something in your program which exposes kids to poetry, pottery, ceramics, magic, fantasy, then create such a course because that is the path, that is the avenue which is going to be more valuable for the individual's self-fulfillment, sense of identity and eventual vocational adequacy than anything else you are likely to teach him.

CHARLES MANGEL

If I may, I would like to ramble a bit and touch on several points that were made yesterday. As the only person on this panel, and perhaps in this entire room, who is not a professional trained specifically for the care and feeding of children, I feel free to comment on the role and work of professionals.

The schools took a beating in yesterday's presentations. For the most part, they deserved it. I love schools. I really do, as we all do. We love the good teachers, and we hate the bad teachers. We love the good administrators and the good principals, and we wish we could get rid of all of the others. In my simplistic view, the purpose of school is to teach. There are no exceptions. The purpose of the schools is not to teach that child who, as so many teachers like to say, is ready to learn. The purpose of school is to teach all children. With so many kids, the schools do need help. Of course, we can't expect them to do a total job. A school district, for example, which has one psychologist for thirteen schools is not going to get much done for its children, and its poor, beleaguered classroom teachers are not going to get much help. Every child has abilities, and it is the job of the school to find those abilities. What else is education for?

We are using our juvenile courts, essentially a punitive apparatus, to handle the behavior problems of our schools. And the juvenile courts make problems worse. As we discussed yesterday, they make criminals out of children because we, you and I, do not give them the facilities, personnel, and motivation to do the job. Our juvenile courts system is designed to take the rejects, the kids defined as untreatable, out of the school system. Interestingly enough, in a recent survey it was found that three out of four juvenile court judges had never seen a single institution to which they were committing children. The judges queried all had served a minimum of five years in their positions.

The court has a responsibility not just to commit but to provide better treatment and training for children in its jurisdiction than they would receive if they were to stay within the community. If facilities are not able to provide that degree of treatment, then children should not be sent there.

In virtually all states in this country, the so-called "incorrigible" child can, under law, be held in a juvenile institution until age twenty one without any requirement for additional hearings or any legal demand that he be represented by an attorney. And at age twenty one, he can be transferred to an adult prison if those who run the juvenile prison so judge.

This may have changed, but when I was doing my research, two state courts, Wisconsin and Ohio, said that juvenile jails in their states were "educational institutions." I visited several jails for children in those two states. Take my word for it—they are not educational institutions in the way we like to think of education. In my own state of New Jersey, which is one of the worst in the country as far as treating juvenile offenders is concerned, we have a law in the books that goes back to 1888 and which is still current that allows people, children and adults, to be committed for life to institutions for such things as "being a public nuisance." There is no legal requirement that a judicial file be kept on that person. Therefore, that person has no legal right to review. We are now finding through Legal Aid in New Jersey, people seventy and eighty years of age who have been in institutions of varying sorts since they were children.

Retarded children are often committed to state jails because the state institutions for the retarded are so overcrowded. They grow old in these institutions and, as adults, often are transferred to adult prisons. About ten years ago in Minnesota, a new Director of Corrections for the state in his preliminary tour of facilities, found several dozen retarded adults in the adult prisons who had never had a hearing in criminal court. They had been placed there for "administrative convenience." It was illegal. He immediately contacted the Commissioner of Welfare who was responsible for retarded adults in Minnesota. He told the Commissioner to relocate these people in proper facilities or he would simply discharge them. Open the gate and let them go! He gave a deadline, and they were removed from the prisons. I call that courage, and I applaud that kind of work. Unfortunately, we don't have enough of that being done by our professionals today.

This leads me to another question. Where the devil are our attorneys? What a force for good the organized bar could be! It is outside of this bureaucracy we've been talking about. Wouldn't it be marvelous if lawyers descended on juvenile courts in wholesale groups with writs demanding the release of kids from correctional institutions, from jails, if they were not being treated? I wonder what impact this would have on the overcrowded conditions.

The juvenile code in my state says that jails for juveniles must provide care and treatment better than that available at home. I am not aware of any institution in my state that does this. I am not aware of any child being released because the institution he is in does not do this. Nor have I seen any interest on the part of the bar to do something about this.

We are in our society "problem oriented." We care very little about prevention. If we went to any probation officer and asked him to show us two or three of his most serious cases and if we traced their history, we would find that every child who is a serious delinquent is a failure of one or two agencies down the line. The lives of many of our learning disabled and allegedly delinquent children are controlled, to a large degree, by government. Government, at any level, vacillates according to pressures of the moment. Elected officials, with rare exceptions, are fearful men. For all their seeming confidence, they worry about reelection, about remaining at the public trough, and their programs and their priorities reflect that single point and no other, and we should remember this. The great mathematician and teacher, Alfred White Northhead, once said, "When one considers the importance of the question of the education of a nation's young, the broken lives, the defeated hopes, the national failures which result from the frivolous inertia with which it is treated, it is difficult to restrain within oneself a savage rage."

May I ask that you interpret education broadly, as I do, and develop and maintain a "savage rage."

SOL GORDON

I admire the work of Dr. Levy very much and agree that medical examinations and medication are important, but once a person is "organized," he still needs to learn how to say hello! Once a youngster is in a better position to learn, he still has to learn, and one of the things I have discovered is that so many people who have learning disabilities don't even know how to shake hands. We've got to teach them how to shake hands. We've got to teach them how to relate to other people. When these kids say that they have nothing to do or nothing to say, we have to tell them, "Look, if you have nothing to say, then listen, because people who do a lot of talking need listeners. Maybe if you listen and pretend you're interested, you might find something to say." We still need to teach them, for example, that when somebody asks, "How are you?" you are not supposed to tell them the truth!

I strongly feel that we have over-professionalized this field. I do very little testing. If I really want to get to know someone, I'll invite them out to dinner with a group of other people. I shake their hands, I talk to them, I watch how they don't listen to me, I watch how they eat, I observe a lot of other things, and in an hour and a half, I've discovered more than I could discover in several hours of testing. Perhaps we ought to remember that the best thing Freud ever said was that the best diagnosis is made at the end of a case. We don't make a good diagnosis at the beginning because we lock kids into things we're not sure about and don't understand.

Let's provide all the kind of experiences young people need, and then let's make the diagnosis, because in most cases we'll discover that what we thought was wrong was not wrong at all. Perhaps we also ought to learn some clues from people. When someone says they don't have too many friends, perhaps it means they don't have any friends. Perhaps we need to discover, also, that there are a lot of things that just plain "people" can do. It's no accident that Alcoholics Anonymous, a group of people who are not professional at all, are the most successful with alcoholics. It's no accident that Recovery, Inc., people who are not professional at all, are most successful with those who have been mentally ill.

The current trend is if we don't like somebody, we describe them as "latent" something or other. When I was growing up, the fashionable latency was that everyone was a latent psychopath. Now the fashionable latencies are, of course, latent schizophrenia and latent homosexuality. Do you know what Thomas says about schizophrenia? "If you talk to God, you're religious, but if God talks to you, you're schizophrenic." I hope you won't let anybody make a latency case out of you. Latency may be all you have, and don't allow anybody to take that away from you.

The most successful experience I ever had was with a group of young people who were diagnosed as un-everything—they were unattractive, uninteresting, uninspiring, they were just "un"! The main thing that was wrong with them was they were twenty-five years old, and they were unemployable. All of them had gone through all of the rehabilitation services, and at twenty-five they had been mis-everything. They had been misdiagnosed, misunderstood, misappreciated. So I had a group of ten people who were "un" and "mis" everything. Can you imagine bringing this group together?

They all looked mentally retarded although not one of them was mentally retarded. We brought them together in a group, and they presented each other with anger and hostility. They said, "Oh, Mary, you're in this group. You're crazy. I don't want to be with *you*." "Oh, Jimmy, are you in this group? You're retarded. I don't want to be with you." That's the way people who are unloved and uncared for relate to one another. That's the way people relate to each other if they have no feelings or concerns about themselves. People who have no good self-image hate everybody. Have you noticed that? The most unattractive people are unattractive. People who are bored are boring!

We said to the group (not according to conventional therapeutic techniques), "Don't express yourselves." You're supposed to say, "Express yourselves, say how you feel, express your hostilities." We said to them, "For heaven's sake, if you can't say something nice, don't say it." We said to them, "First you are going to have to learn to like each other and care about each other." In two and a half years, these twenty-five year old "un-everythings" discovered how to get along with each other and how to care about themselves. There was one girl who was fat, ugly, disgusting, stupid, boring–*I* even felt that way about her! We learned that she was going to have a birthday in two weeks, so we said, "Look, we'll have a birthday party, and we'll have it at your house." It was the first time in her life that anybody had come to her house. She had spent her life sitting around being fat, doing nothing, watching television. She couldn't clean, she couldn't cook, she couldn't sew, she couldn't do anything! But in two weeks she learned how to cook, how to sew, how to clean, how to do everything because her friends were coming to her house for her birthday! Eight out of ten of these young people became employable, didn't look retarded, instead of "un," they became everything.

It is never too late to start!

WILLIAM MULLIGAN

I remember an eight-year-old youngster who was under the jurisdiction of the Youth Authority because he was a runaway. He hadn't been out of trouble for any period longer than three months, and I've often wondered if that wasn't during the summertime when there was no pressure to go to school.

I have heard comments that we came down pretty hard yesterday on the schools, on probation, on corrections. Perhaps we did–and with good reason. As head of a public agency, funded by the county, I recognize that my department has certain limitations. Yet I am convinced that we must continue to fight to improve conditions, and schools must continue to fight for better, more meaningful eduational programs.

Young teachers are now emerging from our teacher training institutions who have some knowledge and expertise in the area of learning disabilities. But many school districts aren't hiring so those young people aren't being given an opportunity to teach and to move towards change. Let's get these bright young people into the schools, and let's work constructively and actively with the resources that we have, and maybe we can do something about the eight-year-old runaways in the land.

ALLEN BERMAN

Dr. Brutten and I happened to be having coffee together this morning, and we started speculating on some of the things we have been thinking about separately and independently, and we marvelled at how, from different starting points, we seemed to have arrived at a very similar kind of speculation. So, remembering his comments about people of creativity and genius and how many of them had early disabilities, think, if you will, with me for a minute about some of the speculations I've been working on.

We have had no resistance in the years we have been studying disabilities and retardation to the idea that the nervous system in individuals who function poorly or who are functioning with some disability is different from the rest of us. Let's carry this reasoning to the opposite extreme and think for a minute about the brilliant, creative person—not just the bright person, but someone whose brilliance and creativity stands out from everyone else. Isn't there every reason to believe that someone who can function at this level with this kind of unusual, unique creativity has a nervous system which, in some respects, must be different from that of the rest of us? If we make the basic assumption that most of our functioning is a result of our nervous system integrity, then we should be willing to make the assumption that a disabled person or a retarded person has a nervous system that is different. And we should be equally willing to make the assumption that a person who is brilliant or exceptionally creative, also has a nervous system that is different from most of us.

Now hold that assumption in your head for a bit while I tell you what I have learned as a non-M.D. but with close association with several neurologists who routinely read EEG's. I have read a lot of EEG's with these neurologists, and I have become particularly interested in those that were run on youngsters who were eventually diagnosed as minimally brain damaged, hyperkinetic, or one of the similar terms used when there is not a more definable syndrome. In a rough study, more than 50 percent of the EEG's of such individuals brought the following kinds of statement by the neurologist: "This EEG is non-specifically abnormal" or "This EEG shows a pattern that doesn't seem normal but doesn't fit in with recognized syndromes."

Can't we put this information together with the kind of thing I described earlier and make the assumption that it is possible perhaps for people to be so unusually creative and brilliant that their nervous system can function differently enough so that their EEG's look different? Yet because we are so bound by the thought process that "different" means bad or "different" means dysfunctional, they get categorized as disabled or "essentially normal" (which means a little abnormal). So I was talking to Dr. Brutten about this, and he was telling me about his speculations, and we marvelled at the fact that they seemed to run together.

We are beginning to plan some research, if we can get funding for it, for getting a group of minimally brain dysfunction or hyperkinetic kids who were diagnosed on the basis of EEG's and for finding a group of very bright, creative, genius-level kids (controlling for the obvious variables) who have not ever been recognized from the start as being brilliant. Get EEG's on them, too, mix them up, take them to somebody who reads EEG's and see if he can tell the difference! I'll be willing to bet my Rorshach, which I've been trying to get rid of anyway for a long time, that in a large number of cases they would be misclassified, that you couldn't tell the difference between the dysfunctional ones who were dysfunctioning in a retarded or in a less competence sense from the dysfunctional ones who are dysfunctioning in a more competence sense. Why does a seizure have to be a seizure of disability? Why can't a seizure be a seizure of brilliance? I think it cries out for the kind of thing that several people have already mentioned—a new need to begin to look at differences in people as manifestations of a uniqueness that makes people stimulating in the very fact that they are different. Let's stop demanding that in order for a kid to survive in a school system, he has to be just like everybody else!

RICHARD COMPTON

Since speaking here yesterday afternoon and in talking with a number of people, I have had several rather interesting questions directed at me. Several of them concerned this term "special education." I get rather perturbed at the term "special education" because, to me, education is education, and I don't see anything special about any of it! Recently, I read a magazine article which stated that the average graduating senior in this country measured on standardized tests at the functioning level of 10.4. If a standardized test is accurate and valid, and your average graduate from our public school system measures out at 10.4, and if you look at the possibility of the median and the number of students who are graduating with diplomas who function at the fourth, fifth, and sixth grade level, as would be indicated by that kind of test result, it makes you wonder what all this artificiality about a high school diploma really means.

In Colorado, our effort in our institutions in the area of learning disabilities is not to treat the learning disability, not to correct it, not to teach the child to adapt to it, but to reinterest that child in learning. He has been programmed for failure for so many years that his self-image is reduced to the point where he won't try to do anything because he automatically knows he can't. If we can do nothing else in the average seven and a half months that we have youngsters in our institutions but get a child to say, "I will try," we will have accomplished more for him than the public schools did in the eight, nine or ten years in which they had him. Then we send him back to public school and in two days he is again saying, "I can't do it."

I am not attacking public schools in general. I am attacking public schools specifically. And I attack them based on several years of personal experience as a public school teacher, principal, and superintendent. Yet public schools are not to blame for what they do because public schools reflect the wants and desires and needs of the community, and if the communities need high school graduates who are functioning at the fourth, fifth and sixth grade level, then they have them. That's exactly the kind of schools we have, and special education is not going to be the answer. To me, the answer is to have child-oriented schools which pursue the kind of philosophy which have been expressed during this symposium. Why do we sentence a kid to twelve years in school and get him to achieve approximately three years above where he was when he started? Why do we make him hate to learn, make him refuse to try, squash all of the creativity and the native abilities which he had naturally to begin with?

I have seen the kinds of institutions described during this meeting. I don't think we have those kinds of institution in Colorado. First of all, we have a juvenile code which makes all sentences indeterminate, sentences with a maximum of two years. No child can remain in an institution more than two years without a special court review, and we have had only two cases in the last five years in which youngsters have remained longer than that. Our average length of stay is seven and a half months. But the institutions described do exist. I visited one in a neighboring state and talked to some of the kids. I remember one girl who had been there for a year and a half and who was certainly not receiving an educational program. (By the way, all institutions across the country became "educational" institutions in 1967. That was when Federal legislation was passed which said Title One funds would be available to correctional agencies which were called "educational" institutions.) As I talked with this girl, she seemed quite happy where she was. I asked her what she was there for, and it was truancy, no crime, nothing which could be considered a crime for an adult. I asked her if she wanted to go home. No, she didn't want to go home. In fact, every time they wanted to send her home, she would act up in some way so that they would keep her there. I asked, "Why?" And she replied, "This is the first time in my life that I have ever had three meals a day and a clean bed to sleep in." Maybe some of these institutions are providing things which the homes and the communities are not providing.

I remember another young lady who was in one of our Colorado institutions for continuous, repeated prostitution. I took time to sit down and talk with her, to ask her why, in an attempt to find a way to change this behavior. After an extended discussion when I finally did ask her why she persisted in this kind of behavior, she said, "Because I can do that, and I can't do anything else!" What kind of society do we have which permits this kind of thing to continue?

BRUCE BURT

This morning I would like to put in a plug for one of my pet projects, something that we're working for in Colorado. It is our contention that as long as you have compulsory education laws, you must have alternative education systems. It's unreasonable, it's unfair, it's not right to force kids by law to attend a school which is not geared to handle their individual differences. Furthermore, it is our contention, my contention, that trying to manifest and bring about change from within the public schools is too far in the future. Perhaps ten years, perhaps fifteen years, and even that is, I think, being optimistic. Too many things are taking place in the public schools today that are not going to change. For example, a good friend of mine is in the high school math department of a small community. He's a creative person, very interested in his students. For the last three years, he's been on a textbook selection committee trying to determine what textbook they are going to put these kids in, the underlying philosophy being that everybody is going to be put in the same textbook at the same level at the same time doing the same thing and getting the same results. Three years to select a textbook, yet look at the educational needs we have right now!

What is desperately needed is alternative education programs in the community, utilizing individualized instruction, with child centered teachers who are truly concerned about children. Such creative teachers do exist. They don't need a textbook. But the bureauracy, the system, stifles this creativity. Federal funds are available. Educational models are available. They work! Put these kids in a program that is geared to their individual needs. Build on their abilities, build on what they can do, don't concern yourself about what they can't do, and you are going to get some fantastic results.

CHARLES WEENING

I would like to read a memo written to foster parents from the New Jersey Division of Youth and Family Services, Department of Institutions and Agencies:

"Juveniles in need of supervision (JINS): A new juvenile code identified as JINS becomes effective on March 1, 1974. The code was defined to prevent children from becoming enmeshed in the juvenile court system by offering alternative treatment programs. Its purpose is to preserve the unity of the child's family whenever possible. The major provision is a new classification of juveniles in need of supervision for those children who appear before juvenile court on offenses applicable only to juveniles such as incorrigibility and truancy. The code prohibits the placement of JINS in "physically restricting" facilities such as detention. Previously, JINS could be placed in detention facilities when a parent or guardian was unavailable or unwilling to assume responsibility for his or her care. With this change there will be an increased need for emergency short term placement for these children and shelter or foster care while awaiting court disposition for permanent placement. The children most affected by the new juvenile code are those JINS who initially entered a juvenile court system for social reasons. These children have been neglected, mistreated or unsupervised by their parents or guardians with a long standing pattern of family instability. Due to these problems, they evidence behavior that characterize them as truants, incorrigibles, and runaways. The Division anticipates increased responsibility for JINS children which presents a real challenge because of our present limited resources. Hopefully, with the support and cooperation of community groups we will be able to meet the needs of these children."

I am very happy that New Jersey passed this code. Maybe it will take some of the sting out of some of the things that have been said about New Jersey.

Learning Disabilities and Delinquent Youth

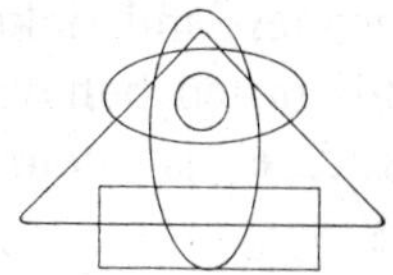

At the time work was going forward on the editing of the proceedings of the "Youth in Trouble" symposium, an article, "Learning Disabilities and Delinquent Youth" by August J. Mauser, EdD, appeared in the Summer 1974 issue of Academic Therapy. Because of its relevance and integrity of content, permission to include the paper in this collection was sought and received from the author.

The Editor.

An abundance of specific social, behavioral, educational, and psychometric traits have historically characterized the delinquent youth; but recently evidence has suggested that today's "average" delinquent is in many instances much different from the delinquent of 10 to 15 years ago.

Today's delinquent is younger. The average age of the delinquent is 13.5 years. In 1969, 39 percent of all arrests were persons under 21 years of age. Fifty percent of all index crimes were committed by persons under 18 years of age, and 22 percent were committed by persons 15 years of age and younger. The peak years for juvenile arrests occur at the ages of 13 and 14 years.

Today's delinquent is brighter. The delinquent of today, with an average IQ of 95, falls within the national norm of average intelligence. The intelligence of juvenile delinquents approaches that of the general population. K. J. Schlichter, in comparing 45 juvenile delinquents and 45 non-delinquents participating in a learning discrimination study, found no significant difference in IQ.[1] In a longitudinal study by Winston M. Ahlstrom, the average IQ for black delinquents was 91, and the average IQ for white delinquents was 94.[2] When today's delinquent is referred to court, however, he has, after an approximate seven years' stint in our schools, evidence of a discrepancy of two to four years between his actual achievement and his achievement potential.

Today's delinquent can be culturally typified. Arrests of white juveniles outnumber arrests of black juveniles by a ratio of three to one for persons under 18 years of age. However, the white juveniles are arrested mainly for crimes involving damage to property, and the black juveniles are arrested mainly for vice, prostitution, and violent crimes against other persons. Summarily, law officers and

---

August J. Mauser, EdD, is a professor of special education at Northern Illinois University, DeKalb, Illinois 60115. ***This article is based on a paper presented to the Tenth Annual International Conference of the Association for Children with Learning Disabilities, 1973, Detroit, Michigan.***

authorities have described the delinquent youth of the 1970's as being a tougher, meaner, and sicker individual than his counterpart of 10 to 15 years ago. Whether this noted behavioral change in the delinquent is related to the so-called "drug culture" is unclear at this time.

The Juvenile Delinquent

Just as there have been classifications and categories of types of specific learning disabilities, there have also been attempts by a number of investigators to classify the behavioral types associated with the delinquent population. In order to truly personalize a program, the worker in this area should be familiar with the various behavioral styles of the delinquent population. One of the earliest attempts to classify the delinquent was reported by E. Hewitt and R. L. Jenkins.[3] These authors classified delinquents as (1) socialized, (2) unsocialized, (3) maladjusted or withdrawn. The *first category* includes those delinquents who are relatively integrated and well adjusted emotionally. These are individuals who will, in all probability, become emotionally mature adults. These children are socialized delinquents and show no symptoms of maladjustment other than the specific delinquent act and the fact that they were caught. Many individuals classify these delinquents as "normal," even though members of this group are repeatedly involved in delinquent acts. The continuum of behaviors of this group is wide and ranges from auto theft for the purposes of joy riding, to committing armed robbery. The *second category* of delinquent has been described as one with markedly weak ego control who is generally regarded as either an insecure person with low self-esteem or a highly aggressive or hostile person. Often times they are openly described as being maladjusted or withdrawn. The literature has often described these types of delinquents as being "lone wolf offenders." The *third category* of delinquent, which appears to require the greatest amount of attention and care, consists of those who have relatively defective super-ego controls and who have not developed society-conforming behavior. They have been characterized by emotional immaturity. Oftentimes, though, they may be socialized in respect to their own peer group.

The concepts of learning disabilities and juvenile delinquency have been separately discussed and investigated often. Both have been regarded by various writers as being "cause" and "effect" concepts defying simple solutions—primarily resulting from the heterogeneity of the youths within each category. Obviously, the youths regarded as learning-disabled and the individuals regarded as juvenile delinquents may be one and the same. Whether one causes the other and holds a priority position in terms of cause-effect relationships should not be belabored. In the future, the rehabilitative treatment design with delinquent youth will very possibly include remedial education components to assist the individual delinquent in overcoming those specific learning disabilities that may be exhibited in his behavior.

The Delinquent, the School, and Justice

There are many reasons why a child commits and is caught performing antisocial acts. Past research makes it safe to assume that some of the reasons for juvenile delinquency may be directly or indirectly related to the child's past or present educational experiences. One of the most frequently cited behavioral manifestations found in the literature related to juvenile delinquency has been truancy. One of the most common descriptions associated with attitudes of the juvenile delinquent has been a dislike of school and the teacher. Specifically, the dislikes have centered on school subjects requiring strict logical reasoning, persistency of effort, and good memory. These educational deficiencies also characterize the population of children having specific learning disabilities.

Many of the children who come before the juvenile court have not been arrested for adult crimes committed against society. They have been arrested because they do not get along with their parents or teachers. The "beyond controls," truants, and those legally designated "Persons in Need of Supervision" today make up over one third of our national juvenile court jurisdiction. Most juveniles charged with predelinquent offenses such as truancy and running away should and can be handled more effectively through short-term intervention crisis therapy rather than through the traditional judicial process.

That a relationship between school achievement and delinquency does exist has been substantiated. However, the strength of this relationship and the reasons determining its existence are relatively unclear. Confounding, too, is the maxim that *not all delinquents are learning disabled and not all learning disabled are juvenile delinquents*. Among the many writers who have cited the relationship between juvenile delinquency and learning disabilities is C. Poremba, who stated that 50 percent of the juvenile delinquent youth referred to the courts exhibited a specific learning disability.[4] M. Critchley found approximately 75 percent of young offenders in France to be nonreaders.[5] In a study of the delinquent population at the Robert F. Kennedy Youth Center, F. Duling, S. Eddy, and V. Risko found that of the children who had average or above-average IQs, 32 percent of this population were identified as learning disabled. When the total population was included, 53 percent were regarded as having one or more specific learning disabilities.[6] W. H. Miller and E. Windhauser cited the possible relationship between reading disabilities and delinquency in secondary school students.[7] Ahlstrom found juvenile delinquents to be three years behind in the basic skills of reading and math.[8] J. Feldhusen cited reading, writing, math, and class rank as being much lower in delinquents than in non-delinquents.[9] Betty Raygor discovered that disturbed delinquent boys had the lowest high school rank, while disturbed delinquent girls ranked slightly higher. Correspondingly, those in the lower track in high school had a greater juvenile delinquency rate than those in the higher, college-prep track.[10]

Both learning-disabled and juvenile delinquent individuals have many behavioral similarities, and following a learning disability model is necessary when assessing, monitoring, and remediating the educational deficits found in the majority of our delinquent youth.

Governmental Concern and Legal Involvement in Programing

Recognizing the need to improve the quality of existing services for the nation's delinquent youth, the Juvenile Justice and Delinquency Prevention Act of 1972 (S. 3148) was introduced by Senator Birch Bayh (Democrat, Indiana) to the second session of the Ninety-second Congress. This proposed legislation was to direct the resources of the Federal government to aid in bringing about an immediate reduction in the rate of juvenile delinquency. In addition, provisions were made to increase the resources related to the improvement of the quality of juvenile justice in the United States, and to develop and implement effective methods of preventing and treating juvenile delinquency. State and local government agencies, both private and public, were encouraged to conduct innovative and effective programs for the prevention and treatment of juvenile delinquency.

Concern with the increasing frequency of juvenile delinquency also prompted action at the state level of government. The North Carolina Law and Order Division recommendations on juvenile delinquency suggest that more extensive educational and counseling programs should be developed within local communities to identify and assist potential delinquents and their families, that additional youth service bureaus and centers should be created, that physical placement facilities for juveniles should be improved, and that aftercare treatment programs should be expanded.[11] Personnel development programs would also be included to offset the great need for adequately trained personnel to work with the juvenile delinquent populace.

Similarities Between LD and JD

Juvenile delinquency historically has been regarded as primarily a social-legal concept. In most states a *juvenile delinquent* is an individual under the age of 18 who is adjudicated guilty of breaking the law. In contrast, the *learning disabled* has been viewed primarily in educational terms as far as output is concerned. For the most part, from an educational standpoint, he has been regarded as a person who exhibits a discrepancy between actual achievement in school and known potential. *The individual's surface characteristics in terms of intelligence, vision, hearing, and motor abilities appear to be normal.* The integration of the modalities in terms of processing information, then, has been challenged. The literature devoted to learning disabilities and juvenile delinquency evidences many similar characteristics between the two concepts:

1. Both the learning-disabled and juvenile delinquent populations evidence a negative self-concept and a low frustration tolerance.[12]
2. Both delinquency and learning disabilities have been problems primarily associated with the male species. Overall, males outnumber females by a ratio of four to one. This ratio decreases to a still significant ratio of six to one when only index crime statistics are used.

3. Directional orientation problems are common among both the delinquent and the learning-disabled population.[13]

4. There is also evidence of a greater occurrence of minimal brain dysfunction among delinquent and learning-disabled youth.[14] Whether the dysfunction is related to actual injury or to delayed maturation is to be questioned. Critchley appears to suggest "immaturity" to account for the differences.[15]

5. The intelligence level of the child with a specific learning disability, according to E. M. Koppitz, is a mean IQ of 92.[16] Half of the learning-disabled population will fall into the average mental ability. These results are consistent with past research related to the intellectual level of juvenile delinquents.

6. Most delinquents and children with learning disabilities tend to have difficulties in school beginning in the primary grades.

7. Juvenile delinquency and learning disabilities appear to have no single cause and no single cure, but are associated with a variety of etiological factors and a multitude of treatment strategies.

8. Both delinquents and disabled readers lack positive personality characteristics and have poor self-concepts.[17]

Treatment Programs

The prevention of the learning-disabled/juvenile delinquent child is the logical and foremost concern. An effective prevention and treatment program must have available information related to the causes of both delinquent behavior and the learning disability. Prevention and treatment are often inseparable. Prevention *and* treatment can be a function of our schools. Obviously, when a youth is incarcerated in either a long-term or a short-term facility for juvenile delinquents, it appears that primarily a "treatment" component is in operation. A preventive aspect is also functioning in terms of deterring future delinquent acts.

From a practical viewpoint, there is a need systematically to mobilize efforts in terms of the educational treatment needed by those delinquents with specific learning disabilities. Hopefully, whatever the treatment strategy followed, it will be developed but not necessarily conducted in a community-based facility. A variety of programing options based on the individual's ability to cope with society is to be emphasized. *The long-term incarceration of delinquent youth, without specific diagnostic and prescriptive components related to his vocationally based academic needs, is an approach of the past and is no longer encouraged.* A personalized treatment program for delinquent children with learning disabilities is needed. The literature is not void of reports regarding comprehensive short-term treatment plans for delinquent youth. The Highfields Project described by A. H. Weeks and the Provo Experiment in Delinquency Rehabilitation described by L. T. Empey and J. Rabow are models which can be easily modified to incorporate the thinking and technology of the 1970's. Both projects contain similar components: they are community based, they are relatively short term, and there is encouragement to participate in the community in both educational and non-educational types of experiences.[18] F. McLaughlin cites 120 girls who are living at the Livingston School for Girls in New York City.[19] Almost all are black and have been convicted of juvenile crimes at some time. The school operates on a non-structured curriculum similar to Summerhill. The teachers stay in their rooms, students sign in and out, and are able to select their own curriculum and classes. Discipline is expected to come from within each child; there is no external system of rewards and punishments. There is no long-range follow-up available yet, but the observations within the school situation point to the growth of greater self-control in the girls and more student involvement in their school. Whether the strategy used in working with delinquent youth with learning disabilities works in concert with educational goals *and* social goals, or attempts to work on each separately with the idea that improvement in one will help the other, is a matter of question.

The School as a Factor

The factors that operate to promote learning in "normal" children often actually retard the learning process in learning-disabled/juvenile delinquent children. According to W. C. Kvaraceus, there are various school associated factors that can be related to delinquency:

> 1. *Good schools must maintain and enforce ordered patterns of living in the daily experiences which they provide all children.* Most delinquents come from homes and neighborhoods which are singularly devoid of any patterns of systematic living.
>
> 2. *The good school demands self-denial, self-control, self-restraint, and a focus on distant goals.* The delinquent personality structure reveals an infantile self-indulging, a here-and-now make-up operating on a strong pleasure principle, and an allergic reaction to the hard-work-and-continuous-effort principle implicit in the learning process.
>
> 3. *The good school presents the face of the benign authority figure.* The delinquent's view of authority is generally negative as a result of the emotional damage and deprivation which he has often suffered at the hands of the inconsistent, disloyal, betraying, and rejecting authority figures frequent since his preschool life.
>
> 4. *The good school tries to retain all youngsters in their school program even after they reach the age of leaving school.* The delinquent child intends to drop out of school and does so at the earliest opportunity, thus conveying his true feelings and estimate of the school's worth.
>
> 5. *The good school remains always the bastion of the virtues of fair play, cleanliness, and good and clean speech.* The delinquent's value system rates these virtues as weaknesses, and finds greater prestige in swearing, stealing, and sex play—all anathema to the school.

6. *The school places a high priority and prestige on the abilities to verbalize and to abstract, which finds best expression through the academic phase of the curriculum.* The delinquent more often than not is lacking in the quality of abilities and interests he can bring to bear on the academic program.

7. *The good school must remain a center for learning and teaching and avoid becoming a community convenience for the emotionally disturbed and socially maladjusted.* Many true delinquents, when appraised emotionally, are found to be sick, and are more in need of therapy than instruction. In a sense, many true delinquents are sitting in the wrong institution.[20]

The Teacher's Role

For the juvenile who is well down the road to a criminal career, but perhaps not past the point of no return, good diagnosticians, therapists, vocational training, remedial instruction, and understanding and sensitive teachers may redirect the future of the child. The teacher or therapist assigned to the delinquent with a learning disability must be someone viewed as reliable, important, and one with whom the child will be working with directly in the educational setting. G. H. Darling has offered a description of necessary attitudes for the teacher or therapist to possess if he is to carry out a supportive role.[21] Although the original description was concerned with delinquent youth, it is interesting to note how the teacher's characteristics and behaviors fit into the often-stated characteristics needed to work with the learning disabled. Specifically, the individual who works with this youth needs to:

1. communicate acceptance both emotionally and physically,
2. expect the best,
3. build and develop the individual's self-concept,
4. establish clearly defined limits,
5. develop the ability to be a "people watcher," and finally,
6. remember that Rome was not built in a day.

Guidelines for Treatment

Previous statements presented by Kvaraceus are as applicable today as they were then. Additional ideas related to the treatment of delinquent youth have been presented by Empey and Rabow. They have stated that:

1. Delinquent behavior is primarily a group product, and demands an approach to treatment far different from that which sees it as characteristic of a "sick," or "well-meaning" but "misguided" person.

2. An effective program must recognize the intrinsic nature of a delinquent's membership in a delinquent system, and must direct treatment to him as a part of that system.

3. Most habitual delinquents are affectively and ideologically dedicated to the delinquent system. Before they can be made amenable to change, they must be made anxious about the ultimate utility of that system for them.

4. Delinquents must be forced to deal with the conflicts which the demands of conventional and delinquent systems place upon them. The resolution of such conflicts, either for or against further law violations, must ultimately involve a community decision. For that reason, a treatment program, in order to force realistic decision making, can be most effective if it permits continued participation in the community as well as in the treatment process.

5. Delinquent ambivalence for purposes of rehabilitation can only be utilized in a setting conducive to the free expression of feelings—both delinquent and conventional. This means that the protection and rewards provided by the treatment system for candor must exceed those provided either by delinquents for adherence to delinquent roles or by officials for adherence to custodial demands for "good behavior." Only in this way can delinquent individuals become aware of the extent to which other delinquents share conventional as well as delinquent aspirations, and only in this way can they be encouraged to examine the ultimate utility of each.

6. An effective program must develop a unified and cohesive social system in which delinquents and authorities alike are devoted to one task—overcoming lawbreaking. In order to accomplish this the program must avoid two pitfalls: (a) it must avoid establishing authorities as "rejectors" and making inevitable the creation of two whole social systems within the system; and (b) it must avoid the institutionalization of means by which skilled offenders can evade norms and escape sanctions. The occasional imposition of negative sanctions is as necessary in this system as in any other system.

7. A treatment system will be most effective if the delinquent peer group is used as the means of perpetuating the norms and imposing the sanctions of the system. The peer group should be seen by delinquents as the primary source of help and support. The traditional psychotherapeutic emphasis upon transference relationships is not viewed as the most vital factor in effecting change.

8. A program based on sociological theory may tend to include lectures, sermons, films, individual counseling, analytic psychotherapy, organized athletics, academic education, and vocational training as primary treatment techniques. It will have to concentrate instead, on matters of another variety: changing reference group and normative orientations, utilizing ambivalent feelings resulting from the conflict of conventional and delinquent standards, and providing opportunities for recognition and achievement in conventional pursuits.

9. An effective treatment system must include rewards which are realistically meaningful to delinquents. These would include such things as peer acceptance for law abiding behavior or the opportunity for gainful employment rather than badges, movies, or furlough privileges which are designed primarily to facilitate institutional control. Rewards, therefore, must only be given for realistic and lasting changes—not for conformance to norms which concentrate upon effective custody as an end to itself.

10. Finally, in summary, a successful program must be viewed by delinquents as possessing four important characteristics: (a) a social climate in which delinquents are given the opportunity to examine and experience alternatives related to a realistic choice between delinquent or nondelinquent behavior; (b) the opportunity to declare publicly to peers and authorities a belief or disbelief that they can benefit from a change in values; (c) a type of social structure which will permit them to examine the role and legitimacy (for their purposes) of authorities in the treatment system; and (d) a type of treatment interaction which, because it places major responsibilities upon peer group decision making, grants status and recognition to individuals, not only for their own successful participation in the treatment interaction, but for their willingness to involve others.[22]

A Final Comment

As an individual enters school and is repeatedly frustrated by the inability to learn by regular class approaches and methods, it seems quite likely that some form of protest behavior might result. Schools should examine children at an early age to detect serious malformations of character and personality, and teachers should be trained to recognize learning disabilities when they are first manifested. Especially in primary grades, there should be a greater number of young male teachers with whom male pupils can identify. School-work should be made more attractive; and reading instruction should be individualized and sensitized to the needs of each child, with special help available when necessary. Delinquents generally respond better with the promise of a reward rather than the threat of punishment. A variety of flexible programs and experiences—curricular and extracurricular—will maintain the interests of each pupil. N. Silberberg and M. Silberberg suggest that experimentation with a curriculum emphasizing concrete experience, realistic vocational preparation, and an attempt at a socialization process within the reach of the child might prove more fruitful.[23] Alternative approaches have been cited which might allow for movement of the delinquent learning-disabled child into the mainstream of society. A bookless approach to education under development by Silberberg and Silberberg relegates reading to the status of an isolated skill to be taught separately, while all other avenues of learning (audio-visual, discussion, etc.) are used for actual education of a child.[24] *Reeducation, as far as is required by employment policies of business and industry, is encouraged, so that a high degree of literacy is not a prerequisite for positions in which literacy is not functionally necessary*. This educational concept hypothesizes that the delinquent youth with a learning disability needs to have alternative ways and approaches rather than the traditional curriculum emphasis in which academic success is equated with acceptability within our society. The community should begin to support the parents of delinquents in their role in the rehabilitative process. As it is aptly stated by the Silberbergs, it is not the talents of the children which require changing, but rather the values and institutions of the society which must be redesigned to accommodate the variety of talents which our children possess.[25]

Juvenile delinquency is unquestionably on the increase in this country. Many of the delinquent youth also evidence learning disabilities. The delinquent youth with a learning disability can be treated but only with the enormous expenditure of energy by highly trained people. Collaborative treatment programs including input from many disciplines is required. Education, law, medicine, psychology, sociology, and social work are a few of the disciplines which have a vital role to play in the rehabilitative process. The delinquent youth, his peers and parents, all must be included in the treatment program. The learning-disabled youth and the juvenile delinquent possess problems different from those of the normal child, and are recognized as needing specialized treatment. The delinquent child with a learning disability presents to us a formidable challenge.

NOTES

1. K. Jeffrey Schlichter and Richard G. Ratcliff, "Discrimination Learning in Juvenile Delinquents," *Journal of Abnormal Psychology* 77:1 (1971): 46-48.
2. Winston M. Ahlstrom and Robert J. Havighurst, *400 Losers* (San Francisco: Jossey-Bass, Inc., 1971).
3. E. Hewitt and R. L. Jenkins, "Case Studies of Aggressive Delinquents," *American Journal of Orthopsychiatry* 11 (1941).
4. C. Poremba, "The Adolescent and Young Adult with Learning Disabilities: What Are His Needs: What Are the Needs of Those who Deal with Him?" in *International Approach to Learning Disabilities of Children and Youth*, Selected Papers from the Third Annual Conference of the Association for Children with Learning Disabilities [1966] (San Rafael, California: Academic Therapy Publications, 1967).
5. M. Critchley, *Developmental Dyslexia* (Springfield, Illinois: Charles C Thomas, 1964).
6. F. Duling, S. Eddy, and V. Risko, *Learning Disabilities of Juvenile Delinquents* (Morgantown, West Virginia: Department of Educational Services, Robert F. Kennedy Youth Center, 1970).
7. W. H. Miller and E. Windhauser, "Reading Disability—Tendency Toward Delinquency," *Clearinghouse* 46:3 (1971): 183-186.
8. Ahlstrom and Havighurst, *op. cit.*
9. J. Feldhusen, "Prediction of Delinquency, Adjustment, and Academic Achievement over a Five-Year Period with the Kvarceus Delinquency Proneness Scale," *Journal of Educational Research* 65 (April 1973): 375-381.
10. Betty Ragor, "Mental Ability, School Achievement, and Language Arts Achievement in Prediction of Delinquency," *Journal of Educational Research* 64 (October 1970): 68-72.

11. North Carolina Law and Order Division, *A Juvenile Delinquency Plan for North Carolina* (Raleigh, 1972).

12. Miller and Windhauser, *op. cit.*

13. Paul S. Graubard, "Psycholinguistic Correlates of Reading Disability in Disturbed Delinquent Children," *Journal of Special Education* 1:4 (1967): 363-368.

14. L. Tarnopol, "Delinquency and Minimal Brain Dysfunction," *Journal of Learning Disabilities* 3:4 (1970): 200-207.

15. Critchley, *op. cit.*

16. E. M. Koppitz, *Children with Learning Disabilities: A Five-Year Follow-Up Study* (New York: Grune and Stratton, 1971).

17. Feldhusen, *op. cit.*

18. A. H. Weeks, "The Highfields Project," *Youthful Offenders at Highfields: An Evaluation of the Effects of the Short-Term Treatment of Delinquent Boys* (Ann Arbor: University of Michigan Press, 1958): 208; L. T. Empey and J. Rabow, "The Provo Experiment in Delinquency Rehabilitation," *American Sociological Review* 26 (1961): 679-696.

19. F. McLaughlin, "Public Schools that Work: Livingston School for Girls," *Media and Methods* 8 (April 1972).

20. W. C. Kvaraceus, *Juvenile Delinquency* (Washington, D.C.: Department of Classroom Teachers, National Education Association, 1958).

21. G. H. Darling, "The Delinquent in the School," *Clearinghouse* 37 (1963): 483-486.

22. Empey and Rabow, *op. cit.*

23. Norman E. Silberberg and Margaret C. Silberberg, "School Achievement and Delinquency," *Review of Educational Research* 41 (February 1971): 17-33.

24. Norman E. Silberberg and Margaret C. Silberberg, "The Bookless Curriculum: An Educational Alternative," *Journal of Learning Disabilities* 3:4 (1970): 302-307.

25. Silberberg and Silberberg, "School Achievement . . .," *loc. cit.*

REFERENCES

Bazelon, David L. "Beyond Control of the Juvenile Court," *Juvenile Court Journal* 21:2 (Summer 1970).

Brooks, Robert. "A Generation of Bright Delinquents," *Times Educational Supplement* 2984 (July 29, 1972): 4.

Closson, Fred. "Delinquency: It's Prevention Rests upon the Academic Community," *Clearinghouse* 45 (January 1971): 290-293.

Frease, Dean E. "The Schools, Self-Concept, and Juvenile Delinquency," *British Journal of Criminology* [London] 12:2 (1972): 133-146.

Glueck, Sheldon and Glueck, Eleanor. *Toward a Topology of Juvenile Offenders.* New York: Grune and Stratton, 1970.

Mauser, August J. "The Remediation of Learning Disabilities in Juvenile Delinquent Youth." From Selected Convention Papers on Learning Disabilities from the Tenth Annual Conference of the Association for Children with Learning Disabilities [1973]. Pittsburg: Association for Children with Learning Disabilities, 1973: 1-7.

Reed, John P. and Baali, Fuad. *Faces of Delinquency.* New York: Prentice-Hall, 1972.

Sacramento County [California] Probation Department. *Preventing Delinquency through Diversion: The Department County Probation Department, 601 Diversion Project—A First-Year Report*, 1972.

Shafer, Walter E.; Olexa, Carol; and Polk, Kenneth. "Programmed for Social Class: Tracking in High School," *Transaction* 7 (October 1970: 39-46.

Finale

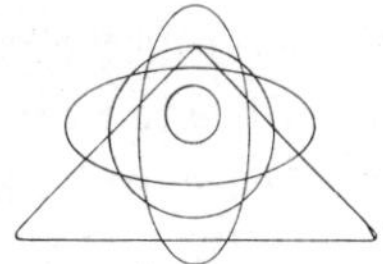

Although I am a judge, I do not appear here today in my judge's hat. I appear here as a mental health volunteer, representing a large group of people who have thus far been basically unrepresented at this meeting.

For the past two days you have been talking about my children and your children and the things that happen to them daily as they conduct themselves in school, on the streets, and at home. Actually, what has really been discussed here is the kind of politicians we all are. Recently, through the national media, we have seen politics in perhaps its lowest form. But I am compelled to say that if what we have been saying for the past two days is literally true–and I believe that it is–then the poorest politicians are not in Washington. If children are our most important resource and if we, together, have joint responsibility for them, then we are the poorest politicians in the state and in the country because we have not communicated the problem to the public in a way which would bring constructive legislation. I am not certain how we step across the barrier into effective action, and I am certain no one else here knows, for if any of us did, there would be a rush to take that step.

The business of trying to translate the type of input, raw information, and resources which we have received at this symposium into a constructive, workable game plan is truly the critical point. That will not be done tomorrow nor will it be done when local state organizations have meetings similar to this. It may never be done. The key question is what will happen under our advice and our consent and our control. We have the expertise to solve the kinds of problems which have been presented here. We have the energy. We have the dedicated people. Yet we are riding in circles.

At every meeting you hear that the problems of juveniles are at the top of the list. There is a time and a flow of history when everything has its opportunity. I submit to you that this is the time when professionals, classroom teachers, interested parents, and volunteer organizations can come together to do something constructive and effective in finding solutions to the problems of children. As an example, I cite for you this beautiful edifice, the world's great airport surrounding us, which was the idea of a single man who got together information and energy and convinced industry and a region that it could happen. And it did happen! The pity of it is that the children of this region are so much more important than an airport. How can we convince the same muscle, the same initiative, the same imagination, that children must come first? How can we rearrange priorities? That's really what we are talking about here in the final few moments of this symposium. I wish I had the answer but I do not.

I can recognize two or three of the basic problems. The first is that we cannot agree on the fundamentals of how to do it. The second basic problem is that we cannot keep our plans open-ended enough to adjust to what needs to be done. The school has a plan, the juvenile department has a plan, the court has a plan, the public has a feeling, and the children get hurt.

I do not understand why we deal in a democracy as if we were in a dictatorship! Let me try to explain what I am saying. What I am hearing from you, unconsciously though it may be, is that you have a great distrust of the will of the people. That is not uncommon. You can call me a politician to the extent that I have more confidence in the general public than I do in specific people. I believe the general public is far ahead of our leadership in recognizing the need to help children, and I believe that the leadership is guilty of malfeasance by not defining and bringing before the public the problems of the children and the youth of our culture.

We know that it is expensive. We know that it is hard to do. We know that we do not really know what to do or what the basic problems are. Yet we have solved such problems in other areas. The will or the commitment to do something about it is the basic problem whether it be at S.M.U., Baylor, T.C.U., University of Texas, University of California, Stanford, M.I.T., or Harvard. We as public people, public officials, judges, legislators, lawmakers, executives, need someone or some group of people to go to the mat, to work with organizations and vested interest groups, to push ideals and programs and plans through, so that, although we cannot have the best of all worlds, we can at least have a beginning.

Classroom teachers need that kind of help, and they can tell us a great deal if we would only ask them. The pity of it is that we are not asking them. Good parents could tell us a lot, but we are not giving the good parents a forum. Public organizations will, in the long run, either approve or defeat your plans and programs. As best I can tell, most of our professional organizations do their best to keep that kind of public opinion out of their inner chambers. I cite for you my own bar association and the medical associations and all those other glorified labels for unions which have closed shops and do not hear the constant, steady, powerful knock of the public need.

Children will be served in our society. Would to God that you and I as experts, as judges, as teachers, as professionals, whatever our expertise happens to be, will be there when their basic needs are met.

Go home and do something about what you have learned!

by
Oswin Chrisman

About the Speakers . . .

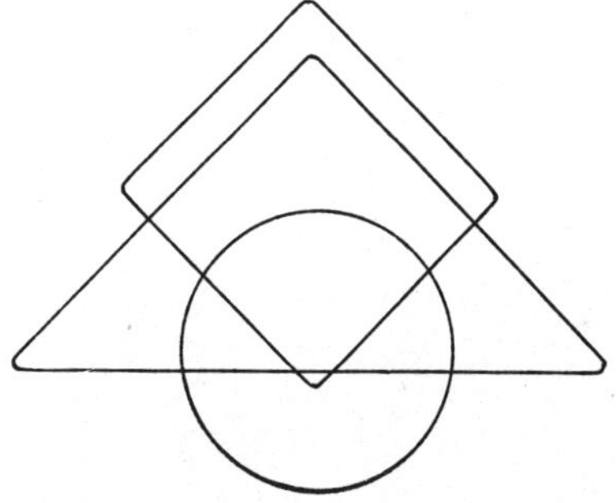

Chester Poremba, Ph.D., *is Chief Psychologist at Children's Hospital in Denver, Colorado. He has served as Chief Consultant Psychologist to the Denver Juvenile Court and, by Governor's appointment, as Director of the Colorado Statewide Planning for Rehabilitation. He has also served as Chairman of the Committee on Juvenile Delinquency for the Association for Children with Learning Disabilities. He is currently serving on the Mayor's Commission on Youth and is a frequent lecturer and author of several pamphlets and articles.*

Harold B. Levy, M.D., *a Shreveport, Louisiana pediatrician, is Co-Medical Director of the Caddo Foundation for Exceptional Children, and Associate Clinical Professor of Pediatrics at the Louisiana State University. He has participated in many learning disability and cerebral palsy seminars, and is the author of the book* Square Pegs, Round Holes: The Learning-Disabled Child in the Classroom and at Home.

Milton Brutten, Ph.D., *a Child Psychologist and Speech Pathologist, is co-founder and Clinical Director of the Vanguard School. He has taught at Bryn Mawr College and Temple University and is Adjunct Assistant Professor in the Department of Pediatrics at Temple University Medical Center. He has served as Director of the Commonwealth Hearing and Speech Center; St. Christopher's Hospital for Children; and Director of the Child Study Department, Pennsylvania School for the Deaf. He is co-author of the popular book* Something's Wrong with My Child.

Charles Mangel *former senior editor at LOOK magazine, wrote "Bobby Joins His World," the first story about learning disabilities to appear in a national lay magazine. For this article he received awards from ACLD, the Education Writers of America, and the National Education Association. While at LOOK, he conceived and wrote articles in the areas of science, education, and social problems, which frequently led to corrective action. He is now a free lance author and lecturer, and consultant to the Child Advocacy Program of Hahnemann and the U.S. Office of Child Development. He is co-author of* Something's Wrong with My Child.

Ben J. Sheppard, M.D., J.D., *graduated from Medical School now known as Lower New York Medical School, in 1932, and specialized in children and adolescents. He was graduated from the Student Law School at the University of Miami in 1952 and was Senior Judge, Juvenile and Domestic Relations Court in and for Dade County, from 1960 to 1967, while carrying on a busy pediatric practice. He studied Adolescent Psychiatry and Family Counseling at Menninger Clinic and Wayne University, and works now primarily in areas of counseling and drug addiction.*

Sol Gordon, Ph.D., *a clinical psychologist, is Professor of Child and Family Studies at Syracuse University and Director of the Institute for Family Research and Education in Syracuse. His extensive experience here and abroad in child guidance clinics has led to specialization in adolescents, with a focus on brain-damaged youngsters. He has written numerous monographs, books, articles, and pamphlets including* Facts About Sex *and* The Sexual Adolescent, *and has made several filmstrips. Dr. Gordon developed a series of 65 television programs on sexuality for the Global Network in Ontario, Canada.*

William Mulligan, *Chief Probation Officer, Sonoma County, California, has been in the field of probation for twenty-one years and has been concerned about the relationship between learning disabilities and juvenile delinquency since 1966. He now gives diagnostic tests to all arrested youngsters. He has described his program to law enforcement agencies and at conferences and has written for various professional journals.*

Allan Berman, Ph.D., *is Acting Chairman, Psychology Department, University of Rhode Island; Chief Psychology Consultant, Governor Medical Center, Providence; and Director of the Neuropsychology Unit, Rhode Island Training Schools. In 1970 he received a grant from LEAA, through the R.I. Governor's Crime Commission, to develop a Neuropsychology Laboratory at the Rhode Island Training Schools for the study of neuropsychological or learning disorders among delinquents. He is the author of numerous publications and major paper presentations on juvenile delinquency and learning disabilities.*

Richard Compton *is Director of Education for the Division of Youth Services, State of Colorado. He has served as Junior High School and Senior High School Principal and Superintendent of Schools. He has also conducted summer sessions and extension classes for Brigham Young University and Adams State College, and has done extensive consulting work with public school districts, professional educational organizations and State Departments of Education.*

Bruce Burt *is Special Education Teacher for the Division of Youth Services, State of Colorado. He received his M.A. in psychology and counseling, and did post-graduate work in special education, testing, diagnosis and prescription. He served as Principal of Lathrop Park Youth Camp, developed and individualized school programs, and helped to develop treatment by objectives. He presented a paper, "Diagnostic-Prescriptive Programming in a Youth Camp" at the ACLD 1974 International Conference.*

Charles A. Weening *is Child Study Supervisor for the New Jersey Department of Education, Branch of Pupil Personnel Services. He is a member of several professional advisory boards and committees concerned with learning disabled and retarded children, and rehabilitation. He is a member of the Board of Hudson County Council of Social Agencies and is listed in "Who's Who in the East." His experience includes rehabilitation counseling, operating with a general caseload of the physically and mentally disabled.*

Patrick K.S.L. Yim *is Judge, District Family Court, First Circuit, State of Hawaii, and Lecturer on Police Science at Honolulu Community College. Judge Yim is a Trustee of the National College of Juvenile Court Judges, Inc., and a member of the faculty of the National College of Juvenile Judges.*

Julius Collum, M.D., *a psychiatrist, is a graduate of the University of Mississippi School of Medicine, and is Medical Director of the Drug Treatment Center in Fort Worth, and parttime Director of Psychiatric Services at the Child Study Center. He has served as Staff Psychiatrist at the Federal Correctional Institution in Fort Worth and as Staff Psychiatrist at the Federal hospitals for drug addiction in Lexington, Kentucky and Fort Worth. His clinical interests include learning disabilities, schizophrenia, treatment of character disorders, and group psychotherapy.*

Oswin Chrisman, *Judge, Domestic Relations Court Number 4, Dallas, Texas, received his Doctor of Law Degree from Baylor University School of Law. He is listed in "Who's Who in American Colleges" and in "Outstanding Young Men of America." Judge Chrisman has served as Director of Children, Inc., as Chairman of the Oak Cliff Chamber of Commerce, and as President of the Senior Citizens of Oak Cliff. At present he is a member of the Dallas County Drug Abuse Study Committee, on the Board of Trustees of the United Way, and President of the Mental Health Association of Dallas County.*

Epilogue

The "Youth in Trouble" symposium was videotaped by Channel 13 in Dallas, Texas, and subsequently televised to 220 educational TV stations throughout the land. The resulting avalanche of letters and phone calls asking that the four-hour program be rerun and that proceedings be published clearly indicated that the problem is as widespread, as misunderstood, as tragic, as the speakers described.

What can be done now—this minute, this day, this year—individually and collectively? A few pragmatic suggestions, based on conversations with professionals in the field of education and juvenile justice, may serve as guidelines:

1. Educators at the secondary level *must* be made aware of the link between learning disabilities and juvenile delinquency.
2. Alternative schools and programs *must* be quickly designed and implemented.
3. New training programs for probation officers, social workers, juvenile judges, and related law enforcement agencies *must* be designed which emphasize the correlation between learning disabilities and juvenile delinquency as well as recommendations for identification and remediation.
4. Parents *must* be made to understand that their child who is dropping out of school because of academic failure may be coping in the only way he can find with inadequate educational placement and unrealistic demands.
5. PTAs and other organizations dealing with children and young people *must* be urged to focus light on the "youth in trouble" syndrome.
6. School board members and legislators *must* be forced into community action to meet the needs—physical, emotional, educational, vocational—of this nation's delinquent population.

It is hoped that the "Youth in Trouble" symposium in Dallas in the spring of '74 will trigger similar symposia in every state. The videotapes and proceedings should be helpful in stimulating interest and awareness and in providing factual, relevant, accurate, current information on the problem at hand.

The Texas Association for Children with Learning Disabilities and its chapters who planned the symposium have a commitment to continue to help, to push, to prod, to insist, to lobby–until local, state, and federal educational and judicial systems finally heed the cry and present proof of their willingness and ability to respond to the desperate plight of our country's "Youth in Trouble."

Betty Lou Kratoville,
Editor

President,
Texas Association for Children with Learning Disabilities